How to Be an Anticapitalist in the Twenty-First Century

How to Be an Anticapitalist in the Twenty-First Century

Erik Olin Wright

VERSO
London • New York

This paperback edition first published by Verso 2021
First published by Verso 2019
© Erik Olin Wright 2019, 2021
Afterword © Michael Burawoy 2019, 2021

1 3 5 7 9 10 8 6 4 2

Verso
UK: 6 Meard Street, London W1F 0EG
US: 20 Jay Street, Suite 1010, Brooklyn, NY 11201

versobooks.com

Verso is the imprint of New Left Books

ISBN-13: 978-1-78873-955-9
ISBN-13: 978-1-78873-607-7 (US EBK)
ISBN-13: 978-1-78873-606-0 (UK EBK)

British Library Cataloguing in Publication Data
A catalogue record for this book is available from the British Library

The Library of Congress Has Cataloged the Hardback Edition as Follows:

Names: Wright, Erik Olin, author.
Title: How to be an anticapitalist in the twenty-first century / Erik Olin
  Wright.
Description: London ; Brooklyn, NY : Verso, 2019.
Identifiers: LCCN 2019001983| ISBN 9781788736053 | ISBN
9781788736077 (US
  EBK) | ISBN 9781788736060 (UK EBK)
Subjects: LCSH: Capitalism—History—21st century. | Anti-globalization
  movement.
Classification: LCC HB501 .W964 2019 | DDC 330.12/2—dc23
LC record available at https://lccn.loc.gov/2019001983

Typeset in Sabon by MJ & N Gavan, Truro, Cornwall
Printed and bound by CPI Group (UK) Ltd, Croydon, CR0 4YY

To my three grandchildren,
Safira, Vernon and Ida

Contents

Preface

This book was originally conceived as a streamlined distillation of the central arguments of *Envisioning Real Utopias*, published in 2010. In the years after that title's publication, I gave periodic talks to community groups, activists and labor groups around the world about its themes. Generally, audiences were enthusiastic about the ideas, but many people found the size and academic trappings of the book off-putting. So, I thought it would be good to write a short, reader-friendly version.

By the time I began working on this, however, my ideas had evolved sufficiently that it no longer made sense to write a book that mainly recapitulated what I had written in *Envisioning Real Utopias*. My focus of attention had shifted from establishing the credibility of a democratic-egalitarian alternative to capitalism to the problem of strategy, how to get from here to there. What I initially planned as a short distillation of my 2010 book had become more of a sequel.

I still wanted to write something that would be engaging to any reader interested in thinking about these issues. But I also found it difficult to write about new arguments and themes without the usual academic practices of entering into debates with alternative views, documenting the sources for various ideas that contributed to my analysis, using footnotes to counter various objections that I knew some readers might have, and so on. My problem was basically that I was writing for two distinct audiences: people who would be interested in the issues but not the traditional academic elaborations, and readers who would feel that the book was not intellectually rigorous without those elaborations.

The solution I came up with was to plan a book with two parts. Each part would have the same identical chapter titles. In Part 1, there would be virtually no references, no footnotes, minimal discussion of the pedigree of specific ideas, and only brief discussions of debates or objections where this was essential for clarifying the argument. In Part 2, each chapter would begin with a one- or two-page summary of the basic argument of the corresponding chapter in Part 1, followed by an exploration of the academic issues left out of Part 1. My goal was for Part 1 to still fully reflect the complexity of the theoretical ideas in the analysis, but to avoid the digressions and academic encumbrances. It would not be an oversimplification of needed complexity. The editors at Verso were enthusiastic about this idea and agreed that when the book was published, Part 1 would be published as a short, inexpensive stand-alone volume, and parts 1 and 2 would be published together as a separate book.

My strategy for actually writing the book was to first write a good draft of every chapter in Part 1, keeping notes on what issues needed discussion in the corresponding chapter in Part 2. I knew that inevitably I would make revisions to the Part 1 chapters once I got into the weeds of Part 2, but still it felt best to get the whole analysis laid out first.

By March of 2018, I had what I felt were solid drafts of the first five chapters. The chapter that is the centerpiece of the book, Chapter 3, "Varieties of Anticapitalism," had gone through many iterations and had been presented in different forms in dozens of public presentations. Chapters 1, 2 and 4 all have a fairly close relationship to what I had written in *Envisioning Real Utopias*, and I felt they were also well worked out. Chapter 4 in particular is largely a distillation of the ideas in chapters 5 to 7 of the earlier book. Chapter 5, on the problem of the state, explores issues I had not discussed systematically in the earlier book but had written about elsewhere, so I felt that this chapter was also in good shape. Chapter 6 remained to be written. It engaged an issue that I had not dealt with in a systematic way before—the problem of forming the collective actors capable of acting politically in an effective way to transform capitalism. But I figured even if I did not have anything very original to say on this critical subject, I could at least clarify the issues in play.

In early April I was diagnosed with acute myeloid leukemia. Acute myeloid leukemia cannot be kept at bay with episodic treatments over an extended period of time. The only strategy is to have a bone marrow stem cell transplant. If this is successful, I will be cured; if not, I will die. The prospects of survival are not remote, but far from certain.

When I received the diagnosis, I contacted Verso and explained the situation. The actual stem cell transplant was several months off—there are a number of rounds of chemotherapy needed to set the stage for the transplant— and I hoped this would give me time to write a draft of Chapter 6. I proposed that when I had completed the manuscript, Part 1 be published as a short book without waiting for Part 2. If all goes well and the transplant is successful, then sometime in the future I can write Part 2 if this still seems worthwhile.

It is now the end of July. It has been a challenge for me to work on the chapter much as I wanted to finish the book. There were periods when I could write with focus and energy for a few hours, but also many days when this was impossible. The chapter has not gone through the public and private dialogue that has always been an integral part of my writing, but I think it serves the needed purpose.

One note on the title of this book, *How to Be an Anticapitalist in the Twenty-First Century*. In the book, I argue in favor of democratic market socialism, understood as a radical form of economic democracy. The book could, therefore, have had the title *How to Be a Democratic Socialist in the Twenty-First Century*. I decided to use the more encompassing term "anticapitalist" because much of the argument of the book is relevant for people who oppose capitalism but are skeptical about socialism. I hope that my arguments convince at least some people that radical socialist economic democracy is the best way of thinking about a realizable destination beyond capitalism, but I did not want the book to seem relevant only to people who already agree with that vision.

Erik Olin Wright
Madison, Wisconsin
August 2018

1

Why Be Anticapitalist?

For many people, the idea of anticapitalism seems ridiculous. After all, look at the fantastic technological innovations in the goods and services produced by capitalist firms in recent years: smartphones and streaming movies; driverless cars and social media; cures for countless diseases; JumboTron screens at football games and video games connecting thousands of players around the world; every conceivable consumer product available on the Internet for rapid home delivery; astounding increases in the productivity of labor through novel automation technologies; and on and on. And while it is true that income is unequally distributed in capitalist economies, it is also true that the array of consumption goods available and affordable for the average person, and even for the poor, has increased dramatically almost everywhere. Just compare the United States in the half century between 1968 and 2018: the percentage of Americans with air conditioners, cars, washing machines, dishwashers, televisions and indoor plumbing has increased dramatically in those fifty years. Life expectancy is longer for most categories of people; infant mortality lower. The list is unending. And now, in the twenty-first century, this improvement in basic standards of living is happening even in some of the poorer regions of the world as well: look at the improvement in material standards of living of people in China since China embraced the free market. What's more, look what happened when Russia and China tried an alternative to capitalism! Even aside from the political oppression and brutality of those regimes, they were economic failures. So, if you care about improving the lives of people, how can you be anticapitalist?

That is one story, the standard story.

Here is another story: the hallmark of capitalism is poverty in the midst of plenty. This is not the only thing wrong with capitalism, but it is the feature of capitalist economies that is its gravest failing. In particular, the poverty of children who clearly bear no responsibility for their plight is morally reprehensible in rich societies where such poverty could be easily eliminated. Yes, there is economic growth, technological innovation, increasing productivity and a downward diffusion of consumer goods, but along with capitalist economic growth comes destitution for many whose livelihoods have been destroyed by the advance of capitalism, precariousness for those at the bottom of the capitalist labor market, and alienating and tedious work for the majority. Capitalism has generated massive increases in productivity and extravagant wealth for some, yet many people still struggle to make ends meet. Capitalism is an inequality-enhancing machine as well as a growth machine. What's more, it is becoming ever clearer that capitalism, driven by the relentless search for profits, is destroying the environment. And in any case, the pivotal issue is not whether material conditions on average have improved in the long run within capitalist economies, but rather whether, looking forward from this point in history, things would be better for most people in an alternative kind of economy. It is true that the centralized, authoritarian state-run economies of twentieth-century Russia and

China were in many ways economic failures, but these are not the only possibilities.

Both of these stories are anchored in the realities of capitalism. It is not an illusion that capitalism has transformed the material conditions of life in the world and enormously increased human productivity; many people have benefited from this. But equally, it is not an illusion that capitalism generates great harms and perpetuates eliminable forms of human suffering. Where the real disagreement lies—a disagreement that is fundamental—is over whether it is possible to have the productivity, innovation and dynamism that we see in capitalism without the harms. Margaret Thatcher famously announced in the early 1980s, "There is no alternative"; two decades later, the World Social Forum declared, "Another world is possible." That is the fundamental debate.

The central argument of this book is this: first, another world is indeed possible. Second, it could improve the conditions for human flourishing for most people. Third, elements of this new world are already being created in the world as it is. And finally, there are ways to move from here to there. Anticapitalism is possible not simply as a moral stance toward the harms and injustices in the world in which we live, but as a practical stance toward building an alternative for greater human flourishing.

This chapter will set the stage for this argument by explaining what I mean by "capitalism," and then exploring the grounds for evaluating capitalism as an economic system.

What is capitalism?

Like many concepts used in everyday life and in scholarly work, there are many different ways of defining

3

"capitalism." For many people, capitalism is the equivalent of a market economy—an economy in which people produce things to be sold to other people through voluntary agreements. Others add the word "free" before "market," emphasizing that capitalism is an economy in which market transactions are minimally regulated by the state. And still others emphasize that capitalism is not just characterized by markets, but also by the private ownership of capital. Sociologists, especially those influenced by the Marxist tradition, typically also add to this the idea that capitalism is characterized by a particular kind of class structure, one in which the people who actually do the work in an economy—the working class—do not themselves own the means of production. This implies at least two basic classes in the economy—capitalists, who own the means of production, and workers, who provide labor as employees.

Throughout this book, I will use the term capitalism to designate both the idea of capitalism as a market economy and the idea that it is organized through a particular kind of class structure. One way of thinking about this combination is that the market dimension identifies the basic mechanism of coordination of economic activities in an economic system—coordination through decentralized voluntary exchanges, supply and demand, and prices—and the class structure identifies the central power relations within the economic system—between private owners of capital and workers. This way of elaborating the concept means that it is possible to have markets without capitalism. For example, it is possible to have markets in which the means of production are owned by the state: firms are owned by the state and the state allocates resources to these firms, either as direct investment or as loans from state banks. This can be called a *statist market economy*

4

(although some people have called this "state capitalism"). Or the firms in a market economy could be various kinds of cooperatives owned and governed by their employees and customers. A market economy organized through such organizations can be called a *cooperative market economy*. In contrast to these two kinds of market economies, the distinctive feature of a capitalist market economy is the ways in which private owners of capital wield power both within firms and within the economic system as a whole.

Grounds for opposing capitalism

Capitalism breeds anticapitalists. In some times and places, the resistance to capitalism becomes crystallized in coherent ideologies with systematic diagnoses of the source of harms and clear prescriptions about what to do to eliminate them. In other circumstances, anticapitalism is submerged within motivations that on the surface have little to do with capitalism, such as religious beliefs that led people to reject modernity and seek refuge in isolated communities. Sometimes it takes the form of workers on the shop floor individually resisting the demands of bosses. Other times anticapitalism is embodied in labor organizations engaged in collective struggles over the conditions of work. Always, wherever capitalism exists, there is discontent and resistance in one form or other.

Two general kinds of motivations are in play in these diverse forms of struggle within and over capitalism: *class interests* and *moral values*. You can oppose capitalism because it harms your own material interests, but also because it offends certain moral values that are important to you.

There is a poster from the late 1970s that shows a working-class woman leaning on a fence. The caption reads: "class consciousness is knowing what side of the fence you're on; class analysis is figuring out who is there with you." The metaphor of the fence sees conflict over capitalism as anchored in conflicts of class interests. Being on opposite sides of the fence defines friends and enemies in terms of opposing interests. Some people may be sitting on the fence, but ultimately they may have to make a choice: "you're either with us or against us." In some historical situations, the interests that define the fence are pretty easy to figure out. It is obvious to nearly everyone that in the United States before the Civil War, slaves were harmed by slavery and they therefore had a class interest in its abolition, while slave owners had an interest in its perpetuation. There may have been slave owners who felt some ambivalence about owning slaves—this is certainly the case for Thomas Jefferson, for example—but this ambivalence was not because of their class interests; it was because of a tension between those interests and certain moral values they held.

In contemporary capitalism, things are more complicated and it is not so obvious precisely how class interests over capitalism should be understood. Of course, there are some categories of people for whom their material interests with respect to capitalism are clear: large wealth holders and CEOs of multinational corporations clearly have interests in defending capitalism; sweatshop workers, low-skilled manual laborers, precarious workers, and the long-term unemployed have interests in opposing capitalism. But for many other people in capitalist economies, things are not so straightforward. Highly educated professionals, managers and many self-employed people, for example, occupy what I have called *contradictory locations within class relations* and have quite complex and often inconsistent interests with respect to capitalism.

If the world consisted of only two classes on opposite sides of the fence, then it might be sufficient to anchor anticapitalism exclusively in terms of class interests. This was basically how classical Marxism saw the problem: even if there were complexities in class structures, the long-term dynamics of capitalism would have a tendency to create a sharp alignment of interests for and against capitalism. In such a world, class consciousness consisted mainly of understanding how the world worked and thus how it served the material interests of some classes at the expense of others. Once workers understood this, the argument went, they would oppose capitalism. This is one of the reasons many Marxists have argued that it is unnecessary to develop a systematic critique of capitalism in terms of social justice and moral deficits. It is enough to show that capitalism harms the interests of the masses; it is not necessary to also show that it is unjust. Workers don't need to be convinced that capitalism is unjust or that it violates moral principles; all that is needed is a powerful diagnosis that capitalism is the source of serious harms *to them*—that it is against their material interests—and that something can be done about it.

Such a purely class interest–based argument against capitalism will not do for the twenty-first century, and probably was never really entirely adequate. There are three issues in play here.

First, because of the complexity of class interests, there will always be many people whose interests do not clearly fall on one side of the fence or the other. Their willingness to support anticapitalist initiatives will depend in part on what other kinds of values are at stake. Since their support is important for any plausible strategy for over-coming capitalism, it is crucial to build the coalition in part around values, not just class interests.

Second, the reality is that most people are motivated at least partially by moral concerns, not just practical economic interests. Even for people whose class interests are clear, motivations anchored in moral concerns can matter a great deal. People often act against their class interests not because they do not understand those interests, but because other values matter more to them. One of the most famous cases in history is that of Frederick Engels, Marx's close associate, who was the son of a wealthy capitalist manufacturer and yet wholeheartedly supported political movements against capitalism. Northern abolitionists in the nineteenth century opposed slavery not because of their class interests, but because of a belief that slavery was wrong. Even in the case of people for whom anticapitalism is in their class interests, motivations anchored in values are important for sustaining the commitment to struggles for social change.

Finally, clarity on values is essential for thinking about the desirability of alternatives to capitalism. We need a way of assessing not just what is wrong with capitalism, but what is desirable about alternatives. And, if it should come to pass that we can actually build the alternative, we need solid criteria for evaluating the extent to which the alternative is realizing these values.

Thus, while of course it is vital to identify the specific ways in which capitalism harms the material interests of certain categories of people, it is also necessary to clarify the values that we would like an economy to foster. The rest of this chapter will explore the values that constitute the moral foundations of anticapitalism and the search for a better alternative.

Normative foundations

Three clusters of values are central to the moral critique of capitalism: equality/fairness, democracy/freedom, and community/solidarity. These have a long pedigree in social struggles, going back at least to the ideals of *liberté, egalité, fraternité* proclaimed in the French Revolution. All of these values also have hotly contested meanings. Few people say that they are against democracy or freedom or some interpretation of equality, but people still disagree sharply over the real content packaged into these words. Arguments of this sort keep political philosophers very busy. I will not attempt here to sort out these debates. What I will do is give an account of these values that lends clarity to the critique of capitalism.

Equality/fairness

The idea of equality is at the center of nearly all notions of social justice. Even libertarian notions of justice, which emphasize property rights, argue for equality of rights before the law. The American Declaration of Independence proclaims, "We hold these truths to be self-evident, that all men are created equal, that they are endowed by their Creator with certain unalienable Rights, that among these are Life, Liberty and the pursuit of Happiness." The idea of equality of opportunity is broadly accepted by most Americans; thus, most people acknowledge that there is something unfair about a child born into poverty having less opportunity in life than a child born into wealth, even if they also feel there is nothing much that can be done about it.

Most people therefore hold some ideal of equality in contemporary capitalist societies. Where people differ strongly is over the substance of the egalitarian ideal. Such disagreement animated a very lively discussion among political philosophers in the last decades of the twentieth century; it was referred to as the "Equality of What?" debate. Is the egalitarian ideal *equality of opportunity*? If so, opportunity for what? Or is the egalitarian ideal *equality of resources*? Equality of capabilities? Equality of welfare or well-being? Here is how I propose we think about equality as a value:

> In a just society, all persons would have broadly equal access to the material and social means necessary to live a flourishing life.

There is a lot packed into this statement. Let's break it down.

First, the egalitarian principle is captured by the idea of "broadly equal *access*" to something. This is a bit different from equal *opportunity*. Equal opportunity would be satisfied by a lottery, for example, but this would hardly be a fair way of giving people access to a flourishing life. Equal opportunity also suggests that the main issue is that people should have what is sometimes called "starting-gate equality": so long as you begin with equal opportunity, if you then squander your opportunities, well, that is just too bad. It's your fault, so you have nothing to complain about. "Equal access" takes a more generous and compassionate view of the human condition. It is also more sociologically and psychologically realistic. People screw up; teenagers can be shortsighted and make stupid decisions; random events and luck play an enormous role in everyone's life for good and ill. A person who works hard, overcoming great obstacles, and accomplishes great things in life still owes much of the success to random good fortune. It is virtually impossible to make a clear distinction between things for which one really bears responsibility and things for which one does not. The idea that in a just society people should, throughout their lives—to the greatest extent possible—have equal access to the conditions to live a flourishing existence recognizes these sociological and psychological facts of life. Equality of opportunity, of course, is still a valuable idea, but equal access is a sociologically more appropriate way of understanding the egalitarian ideal.

Now let's look at "flourishing." There are many ways that philosophers and ordinary people think about what it means to say a person's life is going well. Happiness is one measurement. In general, most people say that a person's life is going better when they are happy rather than unhappy, and also that institutions that facilitate happiness are better than those that impede it. The pursuit of happiness enshrined in the American Declaration of Independence attests to its importance. A meaningful or fulfilling life is another formulation. Some philosophers talk about welfare or well-being. All of these ideas are connected. It is hard, after all, to imagine a person being truly happy if they also feel a sense of meaninglessness in their life.

I use the idea of human *flourishing* to capture an all-around sense of a person's life going well. A flourishing life is one in which a person's capacities and talents have developed in ways that enable them to pursue their life goals, so that in some general sense they have been able to realize their potentials and purposes. It is easy to see what this means when we think of a person's health and physical condition: a flourishing life is more than just the absence of disease; it also embodies a positive idea of physical vitality that enables people to live energetically in the world. Similarly, for other aspects of one's life, flourishing implies a positive, robust realization of one's capacities, not just an absence of grave deficits.

I suspect that in practical terms it doesn't matter a lot whether we focus on happiness, well-being, meaningfulness, fulfillment, or flourishing when we think about a just society. These are all deeply interconnected, and improving access to the conditions for the realization of one almost certainly has positive effects on the others.

The value of equality does not say that in a just society all people actually live equally flourishing lives. Rather, the idea is that all people have equal *access* to *the social and material means necessary* for a flourishing life. In a just society, no one who fails to flourish can complain that the social institutions and social structures in which they live obstructed their access to the material and social conditions needed to flourish.

The *material means* to live a flourishing life will vary enormously over time and place, of course, but broadly this includes adequate food, shelter, clothing, mobility, recreation, medical care and education, among other things. In a market economy, this implies that people have adequate income to purchase many of these things. This does not imply that everyone should have identical levels of income. People have different needs for all sorts of reasons, and thus equal access to the material means necessary for a flourishing life implies access to different levels of income. This is why the classic socialist distribution principle is "to each according to need" rather than "to each the same."

The *social means* to live a flourishing life are more complex than the material means, and any list of these social means is almost certain to contain controversial items. I would include at least the following: meaningful, fulfilling activities, typically linked to what is generally called "work"; intimacy and social connection; autonomy in the sense of meaningful control over one's own life; and social respect, or what some philosophers call social recognition. Social stigma connected to race, gender, sexuality, appearance, religion, language, ethnicity and other salient attributes of persons impedes human flourishing even apart from the way these may also obstruct access to the material means to flourish. In a just society, all people have equal access to these social conditions for a flourishing life.

The egalitarian principle of fairness is a strong one. It states that in a just society "*all* persons" should have equal access, not just some kinds of people. Inequalities in access to the conditions to flourish, as rooted in race, gender, class, physical ability, religion and ethnicity, all constitute injustices. But what about nationality or citizenship? Does the word "society" mean "nation-state" or the social system of cooperating and interacting people? In a globalized economy, the idea of "a" society becomes quite ambiguous. Is the world as a whole the relevant "society" for the principle? This is not an easy question to answer, but the strongest form of the value of equality and fairness would extend its reach to all persons regardless of where they happen to have been born or live: it is unjust that some people, by virtue of the randomness of being born on the wrong side of a national border, have drastically less access to the conditions to live a flourishing life. The implication is that in terms of the value of equality/fairness, people should be allowed to move wherever they like and the principles of justice should apply universally. This does not, however, answer the practical question of what, if anything, can or should be done about this injustice. It may be impossible in practice to rectify the injustice created by national boundaries of citizenship, either because the political obstacles are too great or because the negative side effects of eliminating national boundaries would undermine other important values. But the fact that we cannot solve this problem does not mean that, in terms of the value of equality/fairness, citizenship barriers to equal access are just.

One final issue connected to the value of equality/fairness concerns its relationship to the natural environment. There are two connected issues here. The first concerns what has come to be called "environmental justice"— the ways in which the burdens of environmental harms are distributed within a society. The value of equality/fairness implies that it is unjust for the health burden of toxic waste, pollution and other environmental harms to be disproportionately borne by poor and minority communities. It is equally unjust for the adverse effects of global warming to be concentrated in poor countries, and this injustice is intensified by the fact that the carbon emissions that have led to global warming were mainly generated by activities in wealthy countries. Environmental justice, in these terms, is an additional important dimension of equal access to the material conditions to live a flourishing life.

A second issue concerns the relationship of present actions to future environmental conditions. Do we owe any special consideration to future generations in terms of their access to the environmental conditions to live a flourishing life? Or does the idea of fairness strictly refer to the distribution of access among people alive in the world today? This is an especially salient issue for global warming, where the most serious negative consequences will affect future generations. This future-oriented issue linked to environmental harms can be thought of as a problem of *intergenerational justice*:

> Future generations should have access to the social and material means to live flourishing lives at least at the same level as the present generation.

This is the morally salient issue in environmental sustainability: the main reason to care about the long-term deterioration of the environment is that this undermines human flourishing in the future. It is unfair to future generations.

Democracy/freedom

I join democracy and freedom as values. Often people think of these as rather distinct and even in tension: Freedom is about the ability to do what you want without interference; democracy is about the process of imposing binding rules on everyone. Particularly if democracy is narrowly identified with majority rule, then a majority can certainly impose binding rules that trample on the freedom of people in a minority.

So, why then do I treat democracy and freedom as tightly connected? I do so because both of these ideas reflect a core, underlying value, a value that might be called the *value of self-determination*:

> In a fully democratic society, all people would have broadly equal access to the necessary means to participate meaningfully in decisions about things that affect their lives.

If the decisions in question affect me and only me, then I should be able to make them without interference from anyone else. That is what we call freedom or liberty: being able to do things without asking anyone's permission and without interference from others. But, if the decisions in question affect other people, then they should be parties to the decision as well or, at least, agree to let me make the decision without their participation. Of particular importance are decisions that impose binding, enforced rules on everyone. These are decisions made by states, and for those kinds of decisions all people affected by the rules should be able to meaningfully participate in making those rules. This is what we normally mean by democracy: control "by the people" over the use of the power of the state. But a democratic *society* (rather than simply a democratic state) implies more than this; it requires that people should be able to meaningfully participate in all decisions that significantly affect their lives, whether those decisions are being made within the state or other kinds of institutions. A democratic workplace, a democratic university and a democratic family are as much a part of a democratic society as is a democratic state.

In this formulation, the fundamental idea of self-determination is that people should be able to determine the conditions of their own lives to the greatest extent possible. The difference between freedom and democracy, then, concerns the contexts of actions that affect one's life, not the underlying value itself. Again, the context of freedom is decisions and actions that only affect the person making the decision; the context of democracy is decisions and actions that affect other people as well.

Now, in practice virtually every decision and action a person can undertake has some effect on others. It is therefore impossible for everyone to be a participant in every decision affecting them. It would also be monstrous for a society to attempt to move toward such comprehensive democratic participation. What we need, therefore, are a set of rules that define the socially accepted boundary between the context of freedom and the context of democracy. One concept for talking about this is the boundary between the *private* sphere and the *public* sphere. In the private sphere, individuals are free to do what they want without involving the democratic participation of those affected by their actions; in the public sphere, directly or indirectly, all those affected by decisions are invited to participate.

There is nothing natural or spontaneous about this line of demarcation between the private and the public; it must be created through some kind of social process. This is clearly a very complex and often deeply contested task. The long political struggles over sexuality, abortion and contraception all concern the boundary between a strictly private domain of sex and the body, in which each individual can freely make choices, and a public domain in which people in the broader society can legitimately interfere, especially through state regulation. Some boundaries are vigorously enforced by the state. Some boundaries are mostly enforced through social norms. Often the boundary between the public and the private remains fuzzy. In a deeply democratic society, the boundary between the public and private is itself subjected to democratic deliberation and decision.

Democracy and freedom are values in their own right, but they are also instrumental for other values. In particular, self-determination is itself important for human flourishing. As in the case of fairness, the democratic ideal rests on the egalitarian principle of equal access to the necessary means to live a flourishing life—in this case, to participate meaningfully in decisions; in short, equal access to the exercise of power. This does not imply that all people actually do participate equally in collective decisions, but simply that there are no unequal social impediments to their participation.

Community/solidarity

The third long-standing value connected to anticapitalism is community and the closely related idea of solidarity:

> Community/solidarity expresses the principle that people ought to cooperate with each other not simply because of what they personally receive, but also from a real commitment to the well-being of others and a sense of moral obligation that it is right to do.

When such cooperation occurs in mundane, everyday activities in which people help each other out, we use the word "community"; when the cooperation occurs in the context of collective action to achieve a common goal, we use the term "solidarity." Solidarity typically also suggests the idea of collective power—"united we stand, divided we fall"—but the unity being called for is still grounded in the principle it shares with community: that cooperation should be motivated not exclusively by an instrumental concern with narrow individual self-interest, but by a combination of moral obligation to and concern for others.

The value of community applies to any social unit in which people interact and cooperate. The family, in this sense, is a particularly salient community, and in a healthy family one certainly expects cooperation to be rooted in both love and moral concern. Consider a family in which parents made "investments" in children not because of any concern for the well-being of their children but only because the parents felt they would get a good financial return on their investments. For most people, such an attitude would violate important family values. Religiously backed moral precepts often embody the value of community and solidarity: "love thy neighbor as thyself" and "do unto others as you would have them do unto you." The heartfelt chant of the labor movement, "An injury to one is an injury to all" expresses this value. Neighborhoods, cities, nations, organizations, clubs and any other setting of social interaction and cooperation are all potential sites for the value of community.

The salience of the value of community, of course, will vary enormously across time and space. As is often noted, in times of natural disasters, people in the affected place often come to each other's aid in striking and self-sacrificing ways. What is called "patriotism" in times of war also can be infused with love of country and a sense of duty, both of which are connected to the value of community and solidarity. In ordinary times, for most people, the value of community can become quite thin with respect to strangers in distant places.

Community/solidarity is of value both because of its connection to human flourishing and because of its role in fostering equality and democracy. What is sometimes referred to as a "communitarian" view of the good society emphasizes the importance of social bonds and reciprocities for human well-being. Where a sense of community is reasonably strong, people are less vulnerable, they feel at home in the world, they have a more secure sense of purpose and meaning in life. A strong sense of community is a constituent part of a flourishing life.

Community/solidarity is also important for equality and democracy. It is easier to accept that all people within some social space should have equal access to the necessary conditions to live a flourishing life when you also feel strong concern and moral obligation for their well-being. This is why within families the principle of distribution among children is often close to "to each according to need." The stronger this sense of community within larger political units, the greater the likelihood of stable egalitarian, redistributive public policies. Similarly, the value of democracy is likely to be more thoroughly realized within political units in which there is a fairly strong sense of community. Political democracy can certainly exist in a social world where people feel relatively little concern for the well-being of fellow citizens and politics is entirely organized around interest groups. But the quality of such democracy is likely to be fairly thin, with little space for serious public deliberation about the common good and the search for broad consensus.

There is, however, a dark side to the value community/ solidarity. A strong sense of community can define rigid boundaries between insiders and outsiders. This may foster some degree of egalitarian values among insiders, but it can also support oppressive exclusion of outsiders. Nationalism often functions in this way. Solidarity can enhance the capacity for collective struggle of the KKK as well as the civil rights movement. The positive values associated with community—caring and obligations toward others—can also be meshed with social norms of conformity and deference to authority, which can underwrite oppressive and authoritarian relations within a social group, not simply against outsiders. Community and solidarity can thus obstruct as well as promote democracy and human flourishing. Therefore, while the value of community does figure in emancipatory ideals, much depends on precisely how it is articulated vis-à-vis the values of equality and democracy.

The values of equality/fairness, democracy/freedom and community/solidarity are relevant for the evaluation of any social institution or social structure. Families, communities, religions, schools and states as well as economic systems can be assessed in terms of the ways they foster or obstruct the realization of these values. And, of course, proposals for alternatives must be judged on the basis of these values as well. The next chapter will examine how well capitalism fares in these terms.

2

Diagnosis and Critique of Capitalism

Anticapitalism rests to a significant extent on the claim that capitalism as a way of organizing an economic system impedes the fullest possible realization of the values of equality/fairness, democracy/freedom and community/ solidarity. There are, of course, other criticisms of capitalism as well. Sometimes it is argued, for example, that capitalism undermines human flourishing for everyone —rich and poor, capitalists and workers. The rich and powerful, after all, are also subjected to the alienating pressures of relentless competition and the market. A common criticism is that capitalism is irrational, creating instability and waste, which is undesirable in its own right even apart from the way this harms people in some classes more than others. Many environmentalists argue that capitalism is destroying the environment for everyone, not just distributing the harms of environmental degradation unfairly. Capitalism is also implicated deeply in military aggression through the connection between militarism and imperialism as a form of global economic domination. These are each important points, and in different times and places play a decisive role in motivating anticapitalism. Our main focus here, however, will be on criticisms connected to the values that most deeply anchor anticapitalist struggles: equality, democracy and community.

Equality/fairness

Capitalism inherently generates massively unequal access to both the material and social conditions needed to live flourishing lives.

There are two reasons to object to the inequality in material conditions. First and most directly, the levels of inequality in both income and wealth in all capitalist economies systematically violate egalitarian principles of social justice. Even if one adopts the thinner notion of equal opportunity (rather than equal access to the conditions to live a flourishing life), no capitalist economy has ever come close to that standard: everywhere children living in families at the top of the income and wealth distribution have significantly greater opportunities in life. Everywhere people face advantages and disadvantages that are generated by the capitalist organization of the economy, advantages and disadvantages for which they bear no responsibility. Second, the levels of inequality generated by capitalism are such that some people suffer absolute deprivation of the conditions to live flourishing lives, not simply unequal access to those conditions. Even in very rich capitalist economies like the United States, millions of people live an economically precarious existence; they suffer from hunger and poverty-connected ill health; they reside in unsafe neighborhoods; and they are subjected to the social indignities and stigma connected to poverty. Capitalism perpetuates these eliminable forms of human suffering.

High levels of economic inequality are not an accident in capitalism; they are inherent in its basic mechanisms of operation. There are three broad issues at work here: one concerns the central relation between capital and labor within capitalism; the second concerns the nature of competition and risk in capitalist markets; and the third concerns the dynamic processes of economic growth and technological change.

Class and exploitation

At the very heart of capitalism is a sharp inequality between those who own capital and those who don't. This inequality underlies the existence of a labor market in which the vast majority of people have to look for paid employment in order to acquire a livelihood. Most participants in labor markets need a job much more than any employer needs their labor. The result is an inherent imbalance of power between capital and labor. In a globalized economy where capital can easily move around the world seeking the most favorable sites for investment but labor is much more rooted in particular places, this power imbalance further intensifies, generating a very specific kind of economic inequality: exploitation. Where exploitation exists, it is not simply the case that some people are better off and others worse off; rather, exploitation implies that there is a causal connection between these conditions: the rich are rich, in part, because the poor are poor. The income of owners of capital is in part the result of exploiting the labor of workers.

Competition and risk

Inequality between capital and labor is the most fundamental inequality in capitalism, but a great deal of income inequality occurs within capitalist labor markets. It is in the nature of market competition for advantages and disadvantages to tend to accumulate over time, amplifying whatever initial inequalities exist between individuals. There are winners and losers, and winning at one time makes it easier to win at another. This is true in the competition among capitalist firms, and it is true for competition within labor markets. On top of this, the volatility and periodic crises in capitalism generally have much greater impact on the lives of workers and people at the bottom of the income distribution than more privileged people. The wealthy are able to insure themselves against risks to a much greater extent than are the poor.

Disruptive economic growth

The dynamics of capitalist economic development add an additional inequality-generating process. Capitalist competition generates considerable pressures on firms to innovate, both in terms of their production processes and the goods and services that they produce. This, of course, is one of the great appeals of capitalism, and perhaps the central feature that is offered in its defense. The problem is that this dynamism frequently destroys jobs and sometimes whole sectors of employment. This might not be such a problem if displaced workers could instantly retrain and move to places with appropriate jobs for their skills and aptitudes. But training takes time and resources, and people's lives are enmeshed in webs of social networks and relations that often make it costly and difficult to move. And even when, somehow, displaced workers manage to get retrained and move to where they think they can find employment, there is absolutely no guarantee that the type and number of new jobs available will mesh with the supply of displaced workers seeking those jobs. While capitalist development does create new jobs, and some of these are well-paying, there is no process internal to capitalism through which people displaced by the destruction of jobs are transformed into the people that fill the new jobs. The result is sharp inequality between winners and losers of the capitalist development process. New kinds of jobs are created along with the marginalization and destitution of displaced workers.

The unjust inequalities generated by capitalism extend beyond income and wealth. Capitalism also generates severe inequalities in the social conditions to live a flourishing life. Of particular salience here is access to meaningful, fulfilling forms of work. Most jobs that are generated by capitalist firms are tedious, even when they provide an adequate income. Of course, in any process of producing goods and services, there will always be unpleasant, uninteresting tasks to be done. The issue is the grossly unequal distribution of work activity that is interesting and fulfilling compared with work that is experienced as a burden. Capitalism generates severe inequalities in the distribution of such burdens.

None of these processes mean that in an economy dominated by capitalism, nothing can be done about the inequalities generated by this system. In some times and places, it has been possible to significantly counteract the inequality generated by these processes. This is part of what is meant by what we will call "taming capitalism" in Chapter 3. Such taming, however, requires creating noncapitalist institutions operating on noncapitalist principles, which, in order to reduce inequality, coercively interfere with capitalist processes and transfer resources from capitalism to the state to be used for redistribution, retraining and other forms of state intervention. Left on its own, capitalism relentlessly generates levels of inequality in the material and social conditions of life that both violate the value of equality/fairness and create real suffering in the lives of many people.

Democracy/freedom

Many people feel that democracy, and especially freedom, are deeply connected to capitalism. Milton Friedman, in his book *Capitalism and Freedom,* even argued that capitalism was a necessary condition for the realization of both of these values. And it is certainly the case if one takes a long sweep of history, that the emergence and subsequent development of capitalism is closely associated with the expansion of individual freedom for many people and eventually the spread of more democratic forms of political power. It will therefore seem strange to many people to ground some of the central criticisms of capital in the values of democracy and freedom.

The claim that capitalism harms democracy and freedom is more complex than simply proposing that capitalism is opposed to freedom and democracy. Rather, the logic is that capitalism generates severe deficits in realizing the values of democracy and freedom. Capitalism promotes the emergence and partial development of both freedom and democracy, but it obstructs the fullest possible realization of these values. Five arguments are especially salient.

First, the way the boundary between the public and private sphere is drawn in capitalism excludes crucial decisions that affect large numbers of people from participating in democratic control. Perhaps the most fundamental right that accompanies private ownership of capital is the right to decide where and when to invest and disinvest. The decision by a corporation to move production from one place to another is a private decision, even if closing a factory in the United States and moving it to a country with cheap labor and lax environmental regulations devastates the lives of people who previously worked in the factory and destroys the value of housing in the surrounding community. The people in the devastated community have no rights to participate in the decision despite it affecting their lives deeply. Even if one argues that this concentration of power in private hands is necessary for the efficient allocation of capital in a capitalist economy, the exclusion of these kinds of decisions from democratic control unequivocally still violates the core democratic value that people should be able to meaningfully participate in decisions that affect their lives.

Second, private control over major investments creates constant pressure on public authorities to enact rules favorable to the interests of capitalists. The threat of disinvestment and capital mobility is always in the background of public policy discussions, and thus politicians, regardless of their ideological orientation, are forced to worry about sustaining a "good business climate." The fact that the interests of one class of citizens have priority over others violates democratic values.

Third, wealthy people have greater access than non-wealthy citizens to political power. This is the case in all capitalist democracies, although wealth-based inequality in access to political power is much greater in some countries than in others. The specific mechanisms for this greater access are quite varied: contributions to political campaigns; financing lobbying efforts; elite social networks of various sorts; outright bribes and other forms of corruption. In the United States, it is not just wealthy individuals, but also capitalist corporations that face no meaningful restrictions on their ability to deploy private resources for political purposes. This violates the democratic principle that all citizens should have equal access to participate in controlling political power.

Fourth, capitalist firms are allowed to be organized as workplace dictatorships. An essential power of private ownership of businesses is that the owners have the right to tell employees what to do. That is the basis of the employment contract: the job seeker agrees to follow the orders of the employer in exchange for a wage. Of course, an employer is also free to give workers considerable autonomy in the workplace, and in some situations this is the profit-maximizing way of organizing work. And some owners may grant significant autonomy to workers as a matter of principle, even if this does not maximize profits. But the owner still has the fundamental power to decide when to allow such autonomy. This violates the principle of self-determination that underlies both democracy and freedom.

Finally, the inequalities in wealth and income intrinsic to capitalism create inequalities in what philosopher Philippe van Parijs calls "real freedom." Whatever else we might mean by freedom, it is the ability to say "no." A wealthy person can freely decide not to work for wages; a poor person lacking an independent means of livelihood cannot reject employment so easily. But freedom as a value goes deeper than simply the ability to say no; it is also the ability to act positively on one's life plans. Capitalism deprives many people of real freedom in this sense. Poverty in the midst of plenty not only denies people equal access to the conditions for a flourishing life; it also denies people access to the resources needed for self-determination.

These are all intrinsic consequences of capitalism as an economic structure. As in the case of equality/fairness, however, this does not mean that in a capitalist society—a society in which capitalism is dominant in the economy—nothing can be done to counteract these effects. In different times and places, many things have been done to mitigate the antidemocratic effects of capitalism: public constraints can be imposed on private investment in all sorts of ways to erode the rigid boundary between the public and private; a strong public sector and active forms of public investment can weaken the threat of capital mobility; restrictions on the use of private wealth in elections and various forms of public financing in political campaigns can reduce the privileged access of the wealthy to political power; labor law can both strengthen the collective power of workers through unions and create stronger workers' rights within the workplace, including the requirement that there be workers' councils with a role in workplace governance; and a wide variety of welfare-state policies can increase the real freedom of those without access to private wealth. The antidemocratic and freedom-impeding features of capitalism can, if political conditions are right, be partially tamed even if they cannot be eliminated.

Community/solidarity

Capitalism fosters motivations that corrode the values of community and solidarity. The driving motivation for capitalist investment and production is economic self-interest. Adam Smith expressed this idea in his classic book, *The Wealth of Nations*: "It is not from the benevolence of the butcher, the brewer, or the baker, that we expect our dinner, but from their regard to their own interest. We address ourselves, not to their humanity but to their self-love, and never talk to them of our necessities but of their advantages." Philosopher G. A. Cohen, in an essay called "Why Not Socialism?," adds fear as an additional central motivation within capitalist markets: "The immediate motive to productive activity in a market society is … typically some mixture of greed and fear." In greed, other people are "seen as possible sources of enrichment, and [in fear they are seen] as threats to one's success. These are horrible ways of seeing other people, however much we have become habituated and inured to them, as a result of centuries of capitalist civilization."

Greed and fear are motivations fostered by the nature of competitive markets; they should not be treated simply as character traits of individuals within a market. The CEO of a corporation may be personally generous and make donations to worthy civic projects, affirming the value of community, and yet decide to close down a factory because this would maximize profits even though it imposes great harm on the well-being of people in the community. Workers compete for jobs; employees compete for advancement; firms compete for sales. Competition generates winners and losers. The more intense the competition and the higher the stakes, the more greed and fear are reinforced as individualized operating motivations, which contribute to the corrosive elements of capitalism.

"Culture" in this context refers to the broadly shared beliefs and values of people within a social setting. One can speak of the culture of a family, a workplace, an organization, a community, a society. Cultures are always complex, and often contain quite discordant elements. It is certainly an oversimplification to view the general culture of capitalist societies as simply reflecting the imperatives of capitalism. Nevertheless, capitalist cultures generally affirm two clusters of broadly shared values that are in tension with community and solidarity: *competitive individualism* and *privatized consumerism*.

Competitive individualism consists of a set of values and beliefs deeply connected to the lived experiences people have within capitalist markets: the desirability of being intensively competitive and trying to be better than others; the social norm of measuring one's self-worth through comparisons with others; the moral importance of people taking responsibility for their own fates as individuals rather than relying on help from others; the virtue of being independent and the corresponding stigma of being dependent. In extreme cases, these values get distilled into stark slogans: greed is good; looking out for number one; nice guys finish last. But even when people reject such simple formulations, a central theme in the culture of capitalism is the desirability of competitive striving for success even when this is at the expense of others.

People, of course, generally still hold other principles that cut in the opposite direction—"I am my brother's keeper" and "love thy neighbor as thyself"—and many people act on the basis of these more communitarian values at least in some social contexts. This is part of the complexity of culture: the coexistence of opposing principles and values. One of the hallmarks of a relatively stable culture is its success in accommodating such contradictory elements. A robust capitalist culture accomplishes this by narrowing the social contexts in which most people see the values of community and solidarity as relevant and expanding the contexts in which competitive individualism operates. Communitarian values are fine within families and perhaps a circle of friends, but become progressively weaker as they are extended over a larger population.

Privatized consumerism is the second anticommunitarian element of capitalist culture. A consumerist culture is one in which people are led to believe that life satisfaction depends to a significant extent on ever-increasing personal consumption. *Privatized* consumerism treats public goods and collective consumption as reductions of personal consumption rather than important components of one's overall standard of living and quality of life. This preoccupation with personal, private consumption reinforces the relative indifference to the well-being of others connected to competitive individualism.

Within capitalist societies, greed and fear as individual motivations interact with competitive individualism and privatized consumerism as pervasive cultural forms to create a hostile setting for the value of community/solidarity. Traditionally, opponents of capitalism predicted that capitalism would also generate counteracting tendencies that would strengthen solidarities. This was certainly the hope of socialists in the late nineteenth century and first part of the twentieth century, who believed, following Marx, that increasing interdependency and homogeneity within the working class would generate an increasing sense of class solidarity. The community of workers, then, would be the basis for the eventual transformation of capitalism into a new form of society grounded in the community of all people.

While solidarities do certainly emerge in the working class, these grand hopes were never realized. Instead of a trajectory of working-class homogenization and deepening interdependence, the dynamics of capitalism have produced ever more complex forms of economic inequality and intensified forms of labor market competition and fragmentation. Instead of a tendency toward ever-wider solidarity among the mass of noncapitalists, with only sporadic exceptions capitalism has generated ever-narrower circles of niche solidarity among people with unequal, segmented opportunities in the market. Particularly when these forms of class segmentation intersect forms of social cleavage rooted in salient identities such as race, ethnicity and religion, the value of community/solidarity becomes narrowed and fractured.

The cultural salience of competitive individualism and privatized consumerism, combined with the pervasive weakness of broad, countervailing working-class solidarities, poses a sharp challenge for anticapitalists. While it may be possible for some individuals to find ways of escaping capitalism on their own, any serious effort at challenging capitalism requires collective agency, and this in turn requires solidarity. This has proven one of the major obstacles to transforming capitalism: forging the broad solidarities needed for such struggles. We will turn to this problem in Chapter 6.

Skepticism

To sum up the argument of this chapter: the moral critique of capitalism is grounded in three clusters of values —equality/fairness, democracy/freedom and community/ solidarity. While in specific ways capitalism can be thought of as promoting limited forms of these values, it systematically obstructs their fullest realization. Capitalism generates and perpetuates unjust forms of economic inequality; it narrows democracy and restricts the freedom of many while enormously enhancing the freedom of some; and it cultivates cultural ideals that endorse individual competitive success over collective welfare.

There are two main forms of skepticism about this medley of criticisms of capitalism, even among people who share the core values we have been exploring.

First, many people question that capitalism itself is the culprit for some or all of the problems we have identified. A common view, for example, is that poverty in the midst of plenty reflects a mismatch between the skills people have and the skill requirements of employers, and this in turn is largely the result of technical change. There may be a political failure to provide good training or education, but capitalism is not to blame. Or persistent poverty is the result of the disintegration of the family and a "culture of poverty," but in any case capitalism itself is not to blame. Environmental problems are attributed to industrialization, not the profit-seeking strategies of capitalist firms. Deficits in democracy are mainly the result of the complexity and scale of contemporary societies, not the political influence of the wealthy or the inherent rules of the game of capitalism. The deterioration of community values is the result of urbanization, societal complexity and high levels of geographical mobility, not the competitive forces of the market or the culture of capitalism. And so on.

These arguments should be taken seriously, not dismissed out of hand. Indeed, in at least some cases the causal processes identified by skeptics are relevant to a complete understanding of the issues at hand. The lack of skills relevant to available jobs undoubtedly contributes to poverty; complexity does pose a challenge for democracy; and high levels of spatial mobility can weaken a sense of community. The diagnosis and critique of capitalism does not imply that capitalism is the *only* cause of deficits in the values of equality, democracy and community, but only that it is a significant contributor.

The second source of skepticism concerns the problem of alternatives: people may acknowledge that capitalism is indeed implicated in these problems, but also believe that there are simply no viable alternatives to capitalism, either because proposed alternatives are unworkable and would just make things worse or because, even if in principle there might be a better system, the powers that be are too strong and make it impossible to get from here to there. There is either no attractive destination or no way to get there. Alternatives therefore are utopian, unattainable fantasies.

The rest of this book attempts to address this second kind of skepticism.

3

Varieties of Anticapitalism

Most social change in human history operates behind people's backs as the cumulative effect of the unintended consequences of human action. To be able to have a "strategy" for social change, in contrast, it must be possible to produce desirable social transformation through deliberate, intentional action. There are undoubtedly desirable goals of social transformation for which no strategy is possible, either because the goal itself is not viable—it just wouldn't work—or because there is no way to get there. It therefore may simply be impossible to have a coherent strategy for the emancipatory transformation of something as complex as a social system. This is what Frederick Hayek claimed in his strident attack on socialism, *The Fatal Conceit*. Intellectuals, he argued, believed in the fantasy that they could imagine an alternative to the existing social system and bring it about through deliberate political action. This was a fantasy because, Hayek argued, the negative unintended consequences of such massive social engineering inevitably would overwhelm the intended outcomes. If Hayek is right, the answer to the question "What is to be done?" to create a democratic, egalitarian alternative to capitalism is: "nothing."

Hayek's criticism should not be rejected simply because he used it in defense of conservative political positions.

Any project of deep social change has to worry about unintended consequences. And yet, it remains the case that capitalism is immensely destructive, obstructing the prospects for broad human flourishing. What we need is an understanding of anticapitalist strategies that avoids both the false optimism of wishful thinking and the disabling pessimism that emancipatory social transformation is beyond strategic reach. Clarifying this possibility is the objective of this chapter.

Strategic logics

Five different strategies—which I will call "strategic logics"—have historically been particularly important in anticapitalist struggles: *smashing capitalism, dismantling capitalism, taming capitalism, resisting capitalism* and *escaping capitalism*. Even though in practice these strategies intermingle, each of them constitutes a distinct way of responding to the harms of capitalism. We will begin by examining each in turn. I will then introduce a conceptual map of these strategies that will facilitate our understanding how they can be combined in specific ways. I will argue that one way of combining these strategies —which I will refer to as *eroding capitalism*—offers the most plausible strategic vision for transcending capitalism in the twenty-first century.

Smashing capitalism

This is the classic strategic logic of revolutionaries. The rationale goes something like this:

> The system is rotten. All efforts to make life tolerable within capitalism will eventually fail. From time to time small reforms that improve the lives of people may be possible

when popular forces are strong, but such improvements will always be fragile, vulnerable to attack and reversible. Ultimately, it is an illusion that capitalism can be rendered a benign social order in which ordinary people can live flourishing, meaningful lives. At its core, capitalism is unreformable. The only hope is to destroy it, sweep away the rubble and then build an alternative. As the closing words of the early twentieth-century song "Solidarity Forever" proclaim, "We can bring to birth a new world from the ashes of the old." The full realization of the emancipatory alternative may be gradual, but the necessary condition for such a gradual transition is a decisive rupture in the existing system of power.

But how to do this? How is it possible for anticapitalist forces to amass sufficient power to destroy capitalism and replace it with a better alternative? This is indeed a daunting task, for the power of dominant classes that makes reform an illusion also blocks the revolutionary goal of a rupture in the system. Anticapitalist revolutionary theory, informed by the writings of Marx and extended by Lenin, Gramsci and others, offered an attractive argument about how this could take place:

While it is true that much of the time capitalism seems unassailable, it is also a deeply contradictory system, prone to disruptions and crises. Sometimes those crises reach an intensity that makes the system as a whole fragile, vulnerable to challenge. In the strongest versions of the theory, there are even underlying tendencies in the "laws of motion" of capitalism for the intensity of such system-weakening crises to increase over time, so that in the long term capitalism becomes unsustainable; it destroys its own conditions of existence. But even if there is no systematic tendency for crises to become ever worse, what can be predicted is that periodically there will be intense capitalist economic crises in which the system becomes vulnerable, ruptures become possible and the ruling class can be overthrown. The problem for a revolutionary party, therefore, is to be in a position to take advantage of the opportunity created by such system-level crises to lead a mass mobilization to seize state power, either through elections or through an insurrectionary overthrow of the existing regime. Once in control of the state, the first task is to rapidly refashion the state itself to make it a suitable weapon of ruptural transformation, and then use that power to repress the opposition of the dominant classes and their allies, destroy the pivotal power structures of capitalism and build the necessary institutions for the long-term development of an alternative economic system.

In the twentieth century, various versions of this general line of reasoning animated the imagination of revolutionaries around the world. Revolutionary Marxism infused struggles with hope and optimism, for it not only provided a potent indictment of the world as it existed, but also presented a plausible scenario for how an emancipatory alternative could be realized. This gave people courage, sustaining the belief that history was on their side and that the enormous commitment and sacrifices they were called upon to make in their struggles against capitalism had real prospects of eventually succeeding. And sometimes, if rarely, such struggles did culminate in the revolutionary seizure of state power.

The results of such revolutionary seizures of power, however, were never the creation of a democratic, egalitarian, emancipatory alternative to capitalism. While revolutions in the name of socialism and communism did demonstrate that it was possible "to build *a* new world from the ashes of the old," and in certain ways they may have improved the material conditions of life of most people for a period of time, the evidence from the heroic attempts at rupture in the twentieth century is that they do not produce the kind of new world envisioned in revolutionary ideology. It is one thing to burn down old institutions and social structures; it is quite another to build emancipatory new institutions from the ashes.

Why the revolutions of the twentieth century never resulted in robust, sustainable human emancipation is, of course, a hotly debated matter. Some people argue that this was just because of the historically specific, unfavorable circumstances of the attempts at system-wide ruptures. Revolutions occurred in economically backward societies, surrounded by powerful enemies. Some argue it was because of strategic leadership errors in those revolutions. Others indict the motives of leaders, saying those who triumphed in the course of these revolutions were motivated by desires for status and power rather than the empowerment and well-being of the masses. And still others argue that failure is intrinsic to any attempt at radical rupture in a social system. There are too many moving parts, too much complexity and too many unintended consequences. As a result, attempts at system rupture will inevitably tend to unravel into such chaos that revolutionary elites, regardless of their motives, will be compelled to resort to pervasive violence and repression to sustain social order. Such violence, in turn, destroys the possibility for a genuinely democratic, participatory process of building a new society.

Regardless of which (if any) of these explanations are correct, the evidence from the revolutionary tragedies of the twentieth century is that system-level rupture doesn't work as a strategy for social emancipation. This doesn't imply rejecting the idea of an emancipatory alternative to capitalism, organized around qualitatively different principles, as the fundamental goal of social transformation; what it questions is the plausibility of a strategy that attempts to destroy in a ruptural manner the dominance of capitalism.

Nevertheless, the idea of a revolutionary rupture with capitalism has not completely disappeared. Even if rupture no longer constitutes a coherent strategy of any significant political force, it speaks to the frustration and anger of living in a world of such sharp inequalities and unrealized potential for human flourishing, and in a political system that seems increasingly undemocratic and unresponsive. If, however, one wants to actually transform capitalism in an emancipatory direction, visions that resonate with anger are not enough; what is needed is a strategic logic that has some chance of working in practice.

Dismantling capitalism

From the beginning of anticapitalist movements, there were people who shared the critique of capitalism and the fundamental goals of revolutionaries, but who did not share the belief that a rupture with capitalism was plausible. This skepticism in the possibility of a revolutionary overthrow of capitalism, however, did not imply abandoning the idea of socialism.

While a sweeping overthrow of capitalism, at least in mature capitalist countries, would not create conditions conducive to a democratic, egalitarian alternative, a transition to democratic socialism could be accomplished through state-directed reforms that incrementally introduced elements of a socialist alternative from above. This implied an extended period in which both capitalist and socialist relations coexist in a mixed economy: there would be private capitalist banks alongside state-run banks; private capitalist firms alongside state enterprises, especially in transportation, utilities, health care, and certain branches of heavy industry; there would be capitalist labor markets alongside state employment; state-directed planning for allocations of investment alongside private profit-maximizing investment. In this scenario, there would be no simple moment of rupture in which one system replaced another. Rather, there would be a gradual dismantling of capitalism and the building up of the alternative through the sustained action of the state.

The critical preconditions for this strategy to be viable were, first, a stable electoral democracy, and second, a broad, mass-based socialist party capable of winning elections and staying in power for a sufficiently long time that these new state-run economic structures could be robustly institutionalized. Of course, there would be opposition and resistance, but the belief was that these state-organized socialist economic institutions would demonstrate their value and thus be able to sustain popular support.

The idea of the gradual introduction of socialism from above through state-directed reform had considerable support among anticapitalists in the first half of the twentieth century. And immediately after World War II, this strategy seemed to be gaining ground in certain places, with the nationalization of railroads in Britain, the creation of socialized health care systems in a number of countries, the expansion of state-owned utilities in many places and even state ownership of some industries in a few developed capitalist countries. There was much talk of the potentials of a "mixed economy," and some anticapitalists believed that this could constitute the core around which a more dynamic socialist sector might be built.

It did not happen. The dynamism of capitalism in the decades following World War II, along with the ideological offensive against the idea of socialism in many countries, most notably the United States, pushed the expansion of nationalization in mixed economies off the agenda. The military overthrow of the democratically elected socialist government in Chile in 1973, along with other setbacks to efforts at democratic socialism, further eroded any belief that democratic elections could offer a reformist path to dismantling capitalism. By the last quarter of the twentieth century, far from becoming the vanguard of a new kind of economy, the state-directed sectors of capitalist economies became increasingly vulnerable to attack. Under the banner of neoliberalism, privatization rather than nationalization was at the center of the political agenda, even by some prominent political parties traditionally identified with the left.

Taming capitalism

Both smashing and dismantling capitalism envision the ultimate possibility of replacing capitalism with a fundamentally different kind of economic structure, socialism. In this sense, they both have revolutionary aspirations, even if they differ in their understanding of the necessary means for accomplishing their goals.

It is possible, however, to see capitalism as a source of systematic harms in society without attempting to replace it. Instead, the goal is to neutralize those harms. This became the dominant strategic idea of social democratic parties and nonrevolutionary socialist parties in the second half of the twentieth century. Here is the basic argument:

Capitalism, when left to its own devices, creates great harms. It generates levels of inequality that are destructive to social cohesion; it destroys traditional jobs and leaves people to fend for themselves; it creates uncertainty and risk in the lives of individuals and whole communities; it harms the environment. These are all consequences of the inherent dynamics of a capitalist economy. Nevertheless, it is possible to build counteracting institutions capable of significantly neutralizing these harms. Capitalism does not need to be left to its own devices; it can be tamed by well-crafted state policies. To be sure, this may involve intense struggles since it means reducing the autonomy and power of the capitalist class, and there are no guarantees of success. The capitalist class and its political allies will claim that the regulations and redistribution designed to neutralize these "alleged" harms of capitalism will destroy its dynamism, cripple competitiveness and undermine incentives. Such arguments, however, are simply self-serving rationalizations for privilege and power. Capitalism can be subjected to significant regulation and redistribution to counteract its harms and still provide adequate profits for it to function. To accomplish this requires popular mobilization and political will; one can never rely on the enlightened benevolence of elites. But in the right circumstances, it is possible to win these battles and impose the constraints needed for a more benign form of capitalism. The result is capitalism with significantly modified rules of the game.

The idea of taming capitalism does not eliminate the underlying tendency for capitalism to cause harm; it simply counteracts that effect. This is like a medicine that effectively deals with symptoms rather than with the underlying causes of a health problem. Sometimes that is good enough. Parents of newborn babies are often sleep-deprived and prone to headaches. One solution is to take an aspirin and cope; another is to get rid of the baby. Sometimes neutralizing the symptom is better than trying to get rid of the underlying cause.

Of course, not every reform of the rules governing capitalism, even those that are intended to neutralize some of the harms of capitalism, can be thought of as anticapitalist. Banking regulation that aims to prevent system-disrupting speculative risk-taking and stock market regulation to deter insider trading are better thought of as simply helping to stabilize capitalism, protecting capitalism from its own internal self-destructive tendencies. Regulation of fishing to prevent the collapse of fish stocks simply solves a collective action problem arising from large-scale capitalist fishing. Anticapitalist reforms are reforms that introduce in one way or another egalitarian, democratic and solidaristic values and principles into the operation of capitalism. Such reforms may also help stabilize capitalism—indeed, this is partially what makes them possible—but they do so in ways that also make the system as a whole function in a less purely capitalistic way.

In what is sometimes called the "golden age of capitalism" —roughly the three decades following World War II— social democratic policies, especially in those places where they were most thoroughly implemented, did a fairly good job at moving in the direction of a more humane economic system. More specifically, three clusters of state policies created new rules in which capitalism operated that counteracted some of the harms of capitalism and, to a variable degree, embodied egalitarian, democratic and solidaristic values:

1. Some of the most serious risks people experience in their lives—especially around health, employment and income—were reduced through a fairly comprehensive system of publicly mandated and funded social insurance.

2. States assumed responsibility for the provision of

an expansive set of public goods paid for through a robust system of relatively high taxation. These public goods included basic and higher education, vocational skill formation, public transportation, cultural activities, recreational facilities, research and development. Some of these mostly benefited capitalists, but many provided broad public benefits.

3. States also created regulatory regimes designed to deal with the most serious negative externalities of the behavior of investors and firms in capitalist markets: pollution, product and workplace hazards, predatory market behavior, asset market volatility and so on. Again, some of these regulations strictly served the interests of capitalists, but some also protected the welfare of workers and the broader population.

These policies did not mean that the economy ceased to be capitalist: capitalists were still free to allocate capital on the basis of profit-making opportunities in the market, and aside from taxes, they appropriated the profits generated by those investments to use as they wished. What had changed was that the state took responsibility for partially correcting the three principle failures of capitalist markets: individual vulnerability to risks, under-provision of public goods and negative externalities of private profit-maximizing economic activity. The result was a reasonably well-functioning form of capitalism with muted inequalities and muted conflicts. Capitalists may not have preferred this, but it worked well enough. Capitalism had, in critical ways, been tamed. It continued to exist, but in a less rapacious form.

That was the golden age. The world of the first decades of the twenty-first century looks very different. Everywhere, even in the social democratic strongholds of northern Europe, there have been calls for rollbacks of the "entitlements" connected to social insurance, reductions of taxes and the associated provision of public goods, deregulation of many aspects of capitalist production and markets, and the privatization of many state services. Taken as a whole, these transformations go under the name of "neoliberalism."

A variety of forces have contributed to this reduction of the willingness and apparent capacity of the state to neutralize the harms of capitalism. The globalization of capitalism has made it much easier for capitalist firms to move investments to places in the world with less regulation and cheaper labor. The threat of such movement of capital, along with a variety of technological and demographic changes, has fragmented and weakened the labor movement, making it less capable of resistance and political mobilization. Combined with globalization, the financialization of capital has led to massive increases in wealth and income inequality, which in turn has increased the political leverage of opponents of the social democratic state. Instead of being tamed, capitalism has been unleashed.

Perhaps the three decades or so of the golden age were just a historical anomaly, a brief period in which favorable structural conditions and robust popular power opened up the possibility for the relatively egalitarian, social democratic model. Before that time, capitalism was a rapacious system, and under neoliberalism it has become rapacious again, returning to the normal state of affairs for capitalist systems. Perhaps in the long run capitalism is not tamable. Defenders of the idea of revolutionary ruptures with capitalism have always claimed that taming capitalism was an illusion, a diversion from the task of building a political movement to overthrow it.

But perhaps things are not so dire. The claim that globalization imposes powerful constraints on the capacity of states to raise taxes, regulate capitalism and redistribute income is a politically effective claim in part because people believe it, not because the constraints are actually that narrow. After all, a significant part of the capacity of a state to raise taxes comes from the willingness of wage earners to have their earnings taxed—not the willingness of capitalists to move their capital to avoid taxation—and the willingness of wage earners to be taxed depends to a significant extent on their level of collective solidarity. In politics, the limits of possibility are always in part created by beliefs in those limits. Neoliberalism is an ideology, backed by powerful political forces, rather than a scientifically accurate account of the actual limits we face in making the world a better place. While it may be the case that the specific policies that constituted the menu of social democracy in the golden age have become less effective and need rethinking, taming capitalism through rules that neutralize some of the worst harms of capitalism remains a viable expression of anticapitalism. The political obstacles to a reinvigorated progressive social democracy may be considerable, but this does not mean that the nature of capitalism no longer makes it possible for its harms to be mitigated by state action.

Resisting capitalism

The expression "resisting capitalism" could be used as the all-encompassing term for anticapitalist struggles. I will use the expression in a narrower way to identify struggles that oppose capitalism from outside of the state but do not themselves attempt to gain state power. Both taming and dismantling capitalism require high levels of sustained collective action by coherent organizations, especially political parties, attempting to exercise state power. Taming capitalism hopes to use state power to neutralize capitalism's harms; dismantling capitalism imagines turning state power against capitalism itself. *Resisting* capitalism, as I will use it here, may attempt to influence the state or block state actions, but not exercise state power.

Resisting capitalism seeks to alleviate the harms of the system but does not attempt to capture state power. Rather, it seeks to affect the behavior of capitalists and political elites through protest and other forms of resistance outside of the state. We may not be able to transform capitalism, but we can defend ourselves from its harms by causing trouble, protesting and raising the costs to elites of their actions. This is the strategy of many grassroots activists of various sorts: environmentalists who protest toxic dumps and environmentally destructive development; consumer movements that organize boycotts of predatory corporations; activist lawyers who defend the rights of immigrants, the poor, sexual minorities. It is also the basic strategic logic of unions that organize strikes for better pay and working conditions.

In one form or another, resisting capitalism is probably the most ubiquitous response to the harms of that system. It is rooted in civil society, connected to solidarities of work and community. Often, a diverse range of identities beyond class animates the agenda of resistance to capitalism: ethnicity, religion, race, gender. In its more organized forms, resisting capitalism is largely carried out by social movements and the labor movement. But even when unions are weak and a hostile political environment makes collective social protest difficult, workers on the shop floor can resist the oppression and exploitation of capitalist labor processes and class relations. An intrinsic feature of exploitation is that exploiters depend on the effort of the exploited. And since human beings are not robots, this means that in one way or another people are able to withhold their maximum effort and diligence. This is the most basic form of resisting capitalism.

Escaping capitalism

One of the oldest responses to the depredations of capitalism has been escape. Escaping capitalism may not have generally been crystallized into systematic anticapitalist ideologies, but nevertheless it has a coherent logic:

Capitalism is too powerful a system to destroy. Truly taming capitalism, let alone dismantling it, would require a level of sustained collective action that is unrealistic and, anyway, the system as a whole is too large and complex to control effectively. The powers that be are too strong to dislodge and they will always co-opt opposition and defend their privileges. You can't fight city hall. *Le plus ça change, le plus c'est le même chose.* The best we can do is to try to insulate ourselves from the damaging effects of capitalism, and perhaps escape altogether its ravages in some sheltered environment. We may not be able to change the world at large, but we can remove ourselves as much as possible from its web of domination and create our own micro-alternative in which to live and flourish.

This impulse to escape is reflected in many familiar responses to the harms of capitalism. The movement of poor farmers to the western frontier in the nineteenth-century United States was, for many, an aspiration for stable, self-sufficient subsistence farming rather than production mainly for the market. The utopian communities of the nineteenth century attempted to create largely self-sufficient communities that would function on principles of equality and reciprocity. Workers' cooperatives attempt to create workplaces organized around principles of democracy, solidarity and equality, free of the alienation and exploitation of capitalist firms. Escaping capitalism is implicit in the hippie motto of the 1960s, "turn on, tune in, drop out." The efforts by certain religious communities, such as the Amish, to create strong barriers between themselves and the rest of the society involve removing themselves as much as possible from the pressures of the capitalist market. The characterization of the family as a "haven in a heartless world" expresses the ideal of family as a noncompetitive social space of reciprocity and caring in which one can find refuge from the heartless, competitive world of capitalism.

Escaping capitalism typically involves avoiding political engagement and certainly collectively organized efforts at changing the world. Especially today, escape is often an individualistic lifestyle strategy. And sometimes it is an individualistic strategy dependent on capitalist wealth, as in the stereotype of the successful Wall Street banker who decides to "give up the rat race" and move to Vermont to embrace a life of voluntary simplicity while living off a trust fund amassed from capitalist investments.

Because of the absence of politics, it is easy to dismiss escaping capitalism as a form of anticapitalism, especially when it reflects privileges achieved within capitalism itself. It is hard to treat the wilderness hiker who flies into a remote region with expensive hiking gear in order "to get away from it all" as a meaningful expression of opposition to capitalism. Still, there are many examples of escaping capitalism that do bear on the broader problem of anti-capitalism. Intentional communities may be motivated by the desire to escape the pressures of capitalism, but sometimes they can also serve as models for more collective, egalitarian and democratic ways of living. Certainly, cooperatives, which are often motivated mainly by a desire to escape the authoritarian workplaces and exploitation of capitalist firms, can also become elements of a broader challenge to capitalism and building blocks of an alternative form of economy. The DIY (do-it-yourself) movement may be motivated by stagnant individual incomes during a period of economic austerity, but it can likewise point to ways of organizing economic activity that are less dependent on market exchange. And more generally, the "lifestyle" of voluntary simplicity can contribute to broader rejection of the consumerism and preoccupation with economic growth in capitalism.

Strategic configurations

The five strategic logics we have been examining vary along two dimensions. The first is straightforward: is the primary objective of the strategy to *neutralize harms* or to *transcend structures*? Taming capitalism and resisting capitalism both try to neutralize harms. Smashing, dismantling and escaping capitalism all attempt to transcend the structures of capitalism.

The second dimension is more complex. It concerns the way a strategy is oriented toward what might be called the "level" of a social system. Let me explain this by using the metaphor of a game.

Games are defined by sets of rules, but some of the rules of any kind of game can vary over time without calling the game itself into question. Some rules are clearly fundamental to determining the very nature of a game; they define what game one is playing. We can call these the foundational rules of the game. Other rules simply affect the strategies available to players within the game. Think of this in terms of a sport. Rugby and soccer are two different games. One of the foundational rules distinguishing these games is whether you are allowed to hold onto the ball and run with it. In rugby you can; in soccer you can't. If the international body that regulates the game of soccer decided to allow players to hold onto the ball and run with it, the game would no longer be soccer. On the other hand, changes in the offside rule do not have this character: in 1863 an offside rule was introduced to prevent offensive players from hanging around the opponent's goal waiting for an opportunity. The initial rule specified that a player was offside unless there were three opposing players in front of him or her. The number of needed opposing players was reduced to two in 1925 and finally, in 1990, to its present form: a player is onside so long as he or she is level with the last opposing player (aside from the goalkeeper). These changes in the rules certainly affected the possible moves in the game by players, but they did not change the basic nature of the game itself.

Now, think of society as a game: social conflicts can occur over what game to play, over the variable rules of the game or over moves within a specific set of rules. This is illustrated in Table 1 for conflicts within and over capitalism. Conflicts over what game to play are revolutionary versus counterrevolutionary politics. The stakes focus on whether we are playing the game of capitalism or socialism. Within the game of capitalism, reformist versus reactionary politics constitute conflicts over the variable rules of the game. The stakes then concern what kind of capitalism shall dominate the economic system—for example, social democratic capitalism with rules that reduce risk and vulnerability and protect the collective organization of workers, or neoliberal capitalism, with rules that protect corporate power, prevent redistributive state interventions in the market and reduce the production of public goods.

Finally, conflicts over the moves in the game are mundane, interest-group politics, in which individuals and collectivities adopt strategies in pursuit of their economic interests, taking the existing rules of the game as fixed.

The triplet games/rules/moves corresponds to what can be called three logics of social transformation: ruptural transformations, symbiotic transformations and interstitial transformations. Ruptural transformations involve discontinuities in social structures, a rapid break in the nature of the game being played. Symbiotic transformations are more complex; they involve changes in the rules of a social system that simultaneously make the system run more smoothly and expand the space for subsequent transformations. Finally, interstitial transformations result from the cumulative effect of moves within existing rules of the game.

Now, back to the five strategic logics of anticapitalism. Smashing capitalism is a strategy defined at the level of choosing which game to play; taming and dismantling

Table 1. A game metaphor for political conflicts within and over capitalism

Game metaphor	Form of political conflict	Stakes in the conflict	Logic of transformation
What game to play	Revolutionary versus counter-revolutionary	Capitalism versus socialism	Ruptural
Rules of the game	Reformist versus reactionary	Varieties of capitalism	Symbiotic
Moves in the game	Interest group politics	Immediate economic interests	Interstitial

Source: Adapted from Robert Alford and Roger Friedland, *The Powers of Theory: Capitalism, the State, and Democracy* (Cambridge University Press, 1985), 6–11.

capitalism are defined in terms of the rules of the game; and resisting and escaping capitalism operate at the level of moves in the game. Putting the two dimensions together, we get the typology in Table 2.

Table 2. Typology of anticapitalist strategies

		Objective of struggle	
		Neutralizing harms	Transcending structures
Level of the System	The game itself		*Smashing*
	Rules of the game	*Taming*	*Dismantling*
	Moves in the game	*Resisting*	*Escaping*

Actual historical social and political movements, of course, do not confine themselves to single cells in this typology. In the twentieth century, revolutionary communists explicitly advocated combining resisting capitalism with smashing capitalism. Communist militants were encouraged to participate actively within the labor movement on the belief that this was an essential part of building working-class solidarity and transforming working-class consciousness. The strategy was still ultimately directed toward a system-rupture organized through the control of state power, but an essential part of the process through which this was thought to become eventually possible "when the time was ripe" was vigorous Communist Party involvement in militant resistance to capitalism within the labor movement.

Democratic socialism abandoned the idea of smashing capitalism, but still sought a strategy of ultimately transcending its structures by gradually dismantling capitalism. The strategic configuration combined reforms to neutralize harms from capitalism with efforts at building a strong state sector and supporting the labor movement.

Social democracy also involves resisting capitalism, but combining it with taming capitalism while largely abandoning efforts at dismantling the existing system. Here, the labor movement was organized alongside social democratic parties. Sometimes, indeed, this connection took the form of social democratic parties being in practice the political arm of the labor movement. Much of the progressive reformism of social democracy came from the influence of the labor movement on social democratic politics, and one of the reasons for the decline of anticapitalism within social democracy is the decay of labor militancy in resisting capitalism.

Sometimes social democratic parties have had strong left wings with political aspirations to go beyond taming capitalism toward dismantling capitalism. This was the case in Sweden in the early 1970s, when left social democrats proposed a policy, called the Meidner Plan (named after Swedish economist Rudolf Meidner), through which Swedish labor unions, over an extended period of time, would become the majority share owners of Swedish corporations. This was indeed a strategy of dismantling some of the power of capital. The plan, in its radical form, was politically defeated, and the Swedish Social Democrats retreated to the safer parameters of taming capitalism.

Anarchist-inflected social movements responding to the harms of capitalism often only resist capitalism in a defensive response to its depredations, but sometimes resistance is combined with practices that attempt to build alternatives to capitalist relations. In the nineteenth century, cooperatives and mutual societies often emerged in the context of resistance to capitalism, and in contemporary times the social and solidarity economy has also often been fostered by social movements. In some cases, such as the landless peasant movement in Brazil, invading unused land and building alternative economic structures becomes the central tool of resistance itself.

These four configurations were the main strategic responses to injustice and oppression in capitalist societies in the twentieth century. By the end of the century, the first two of these had all but disappeared from the political landscape, at least in developed capitalist countries. Revolutionary communism lacked credibility because of the collapse of regimes attempting ruptural strategies for dismantling capitalism, and democratic socialism was marginalized because of the repeated failure to sustain an electoral strategy that built a state socialist sector within capitalist economies. Social democracy in developed capitalist countries, too, has declined, if not disappeared, and largely lost its connection to labor militancy. The most dynamic form of anticapitalism in the first decades of the twenty-first century has been anchored in social movements, often with strong anarchist currents, that continue to pronounce that "another world is possible." Mostly such resistance to capitalism has been disconnected from an overarching political project directed at state power and thus from political parties. However, in at least some of the movements opposing capitalism in Latin America and southern Europe, the beginnings of a new strategic idea may be emerging that combines the bottom-up, civil society–centered initiatives of resisting and escaping capitalism with the top-down, state-centered strategy of taming and dismantling capitalism. This new strategic configuration, which can be termed *eroding capitalism*, is illustrated in Table 3.

Table 3. Eroding capitalism

		Objective of struggle	
		Neutralizing harms	Transcending structures
Level of the System	The game itself		*Smashing*
	Rules of the game	*Taming*	*Dismantling*
	Moves in the game	*Resisting*	*Escaping*

Eroding capitalism

While the strategic idea of eroding capitalism is some-times implicit in social and political struggles, it is not generally foregrounded as the central organizing principle of a response to social injustice. Here is the underlying reasoning:

The strategy of erosion is grounded in a particu-lar understanding of the concept of economic systems. Consider capitalism. No economy has ever been—or ever could be—purely capitalist. Capitalism is defined by the combination of market exchange with private ownership of the means of production and the employment of wage earners recruited through a labor market. Existing eco-nomic systems combine capitalism with a host of other ways of organizing the production and distribution of goods and services: directly by states; within the intimate relations of families to meet the needs of their members; through community-based networks and organizations in what is often called the social and solidarity economy; by cooperatives owned and governed democratically by their members; though nonprofit market-oriented organizations; through peer-to-peer networks engaged in collaborative production processes; and many other possibilities. Some of these ways of organizing economic activities can be thought of as hybrids, combining capitalist and noncapitalist elements; some are entirely noncapitalist; and some are anticapitalist. To return to our game metaphor, in real economic systems a variety of different games are being played simultaneously, each with their own rules and moves. We call such a complex economic system "capitalist" when it is the case that capitalism is dominant in determining the economic conditions of life and access to a livelihood for most people. That dominance is immensely destructive. One way to challenge capitalism is to build more democratic, egalitarian, participatory economic relations where possible in the spaces and cracks within this complex system. The idea of eroding capitalism imagines that these alternatives have the potential, in the long run, to become sufficiently prominent in the lives of individuals and communities that capitalism could eventually be displaced from its dominant role in the system.

A loose analogy with an ecosystem in nature might help clarify this idea. Think of a lake. A lake consists of water in a landscape, with particular kinds of soil, terrain, water sources and climate. An array of fish and other creatures live in its water and various kinds of plants grow in and around it. Collectively, all of these elements constitute the natural ecosystem of the lake. This is a "system" in that everything affects everything else within it, but it is not like the system of a single organism in which all of the parts are functionally connected in a coherent, tightly integrated whole. Social systems, in general, are better thought of as ecosystems of loosely connected interacting parts rather than as organisms in which all of the parts serve a function. In such an ecosystem, it is possible to introduce an alien species of fish not "naturally" found in the lake. Some alien species will instantly get gobbled up. Others may survive in some small niche in the lake, but not change much about daily life in the ecosystem. But occasionally an alien species may thrive and eventually displace the dominant species. The strategic vision of eroding capitalism imagines introducing the most vigorous varieties of emancipatory species of noncapitalist economic activity into the ecosystem of capitalism, nurturing their development by protecting their niches and figuring out ways of expanding their habitats. The ultimate hope is that eventually these alien species can spill out of their narrow niches and transform the character of the ecosystem as a whole.

This way of thinking about the process of transcending capitalism is rather like the typical stylized story told about the transition from precapitalist feudal societies in Europe to capitalism. Within feudal economies in the late medieval period, proto-capitalist relations and practices emerged, especially in the cities. Initially this involved merchant trading, guild-regulated artisanal production, and banking. These forms of economic activity filled niches and were often quite useful for feudal elites. Within those niches, the economic game was played by very different rules from the dominant feudalism. As the scope of these market activities expanded, they gradually became more capitalist in character and, in some places, corroded the established feudal domination of the economy as a whole. Through a long, meandering process over several centuries, feudal structures ceased to dominate the economic life of some corners of Europe; feudalism had eroded. This process may have been punctuated by political upheavals and even revolutions, but rather than constituting a rupture in economic structures, these political events generally served more to ratify and rationalize changes that had already taken place within the socioeconomic structure.

The strategic vision of eroding capitalism sees the process of displacing capitalism from its dominant economic role in a similar way. Alternative, noncapitalist economic activities, embodying democratic and egalitarian relations, emerge in the niches where possible within an economy dominated by capitalism. These activities grow over time, both spontaneously and as a result of deliberate strategy. Some of these emerge as adaptations and initiatives from below within communities. Others are actively organized or sponsored by the state from above to solve practical problems. These alternative economic relations constitute the building blocks of an economic structure whose relations of production are characterized by democracy, equality and solidarity. Struggles involving the state take place, sometimes to protect these spaces, other times to facilitate new possibilities. Periodically, those engaged in these struggles encounter structural "limits of possibility"; to go beyond these points may require more intense political mobilization directed at changing critical features of the "rules of the game" within which capitalism functions. Often the mobilizations fail, but at least sometimes conditions are ripe for such changes and the limits of possibility expand. Eventually, the cumulative effect of this interplay between changes from above and initiatives from below may reach a point where the socialist relations created within the economic ecosystem become sufficiently prominent in the lives of individuals and communities that capitalism can no longer be said to be dominant.

This strategic complex combines the progressive social democratic and democratic socialist vision of changing, from above, the rules of the game within which capitalism operates in order to neutralize its worst harms and create alternatives anchored in the state, with more anarchist visions of creating, from below, new economic relations that embody emancipatory aspirations. No political movement explicitly embraces this strategic complex of resisting, taming, dismantling and escaping capitalism in order to erode, over the long term, its dominance. But impulses in this direction can be found in political parties that have close ties to progressive social movements, such as Syriza in Greece and Podemos in Spain. Eroding capitalism might also resonate with youthful currents within some established center-left parties—for example, Bernie Sanders's supporters in the Democratic Party during the 2016 American presidential election or the Corbyn forces within the British Labour Party.

As a strategic vision, eroding capitalism is both enticing and far-fetched. It is enticing because it suggests that even when the state seems quite uncongenial to advances in social justice and emancipatory social change, there is still much that can be done. We can get on with the business of building a new world, not from the ashes of the old, but within the interstices of the old. We can build what I call "real utopias," pieces of the emancipatory destination beyond capitalism within a society still dominated by capitalism. It is far-fetched because it seems wildly implausible that the accumulation of emancipatory economic spaces within an economy dominated by capitalism could ever really erode and displace capitalism, given the immense power and wealth of large capitalist corporations and the dependency of most people's livelihoods on the smooth functioning of the capitalist market. Surely if noncapitalist emancipatory forms of economic activities and relations ever grew to the point of threatening the dominance of capitalism, they would simply be crushed.

In order to show that eroding capitalism is not simply a fantasy, the following chapters will address three issues.

First, we need to put more substance into the idea of an emancipatory alternative to capitalism. It is not enough to just invoke the values we want to see embodied in alternatives; we also need to have a clearheaded idea of their alternative building blocks. Chapter 4 discusses the basic contours of an emancipatory destination beyond capitalism.

Second, we need to contend with the problem of the state. As a strategic idea, eroding capitalism combines using the state in ways that sustain spaces for building emancipatory alternatives with a wide range of initiatives from below to fill those spaces. But if the capitalist state is designed in such a way as to systematically protect capitalism from any threats, how is this possible? Chapter 5 examines how, in spite of its in-built class biases, it is possible to create new rules of the game through the capitalist state that can facilitate the expansion of emancipatory noncapitalist relations that point beyond capitalism.

Third, eroding capitalism, like any strategy, needs collective actors. Strategies don't just happen; they are adopted by people in organizations, parties and movements. Where are the collective actors for eroding capitalism? In classical Marxism, "the working class" was seen as the collective actor capable of challenging capitalism. Is there a plausible scenario through which the social forces needed pursue a strategy of eroding capitalism can be constructed? Chapter 6 will explore this problem.

4

A Destination beyond Capitalism: Socialism as Economic Democracy

It is always simpler to criticize the existing state of affairs than to propose a credible alternative. This is why the names for social protest movements so often have the prefix "anti." Antiwar mobilizations oppose a war. Anti-austerity protests oppose budget cuts. Antiglobalization protests oppose the neoliberal policies of global capitalist integration with rules favorable to multinational corporations and global finance. And even when a movement is named by its positive aspirations—the civil rights movement, the environmental movement, the women's movement—the demands are often framed primarily as the end to something: the end to Jim Crow laws; the end to housing discrimination; the end to racial profiling by police; the end to fracking; the end to gender discrimination in employment; the end to restrictions on marriage for homosexual couples.

The issue here is not that the people involved in such movements do not have strong commitments to positive values or hopes for a very different kind of social world. The 1960s civil rights movement in the United States deeply embodied the emancipatory values of equality, democracy and community. The problem is that it is much more difficult to formulate unifying demands around positive alternatives than around dismantling existing oppressive arrangements. In the US civil rights movement, it was clear what it meant to demand the end of segregation laws; it was much less clear what it meant to demand new policies and inclusive institutions that would provide good jobs for everyone, end poverty and empower ordinary people. Once the civil rights movement in the 1960s shifted from an almost exclusive focus on antidiscrimination and equal rights to a positive equality agenda around questions of power and economic opportunity, and began to articulate the necessity of alternative institutions to accomplish these goals, the unity of the movement crumbled.

Until the final decades of the twentieth century, radical anticapitalists had a pretty clear idea of the desirable alternative to capitalism. They called it "socialism." Disagreements among self-declared socialists were much sharper over how to get from here to there—was a revolutionary rupture needed or could the transformation take place gradually through reforms?—than over the central institutions of the destination. Broadly speaking, socialism was understood as an economic system in which private ownership was replaced by state ownership of the principal means of production, and markets were replaced by some form of comprehensive planning oriented to meet needs rather than maximize profits. Of course, there were many details to be worked out, and sometimes ideas about such details could become sources of great contention, but the basic contours of socialism as an alternative to capitalism seemed clear enough.

By the end of the twentieth century, few critics of capitalism retained much confidence in such a highly statist understanding of a desirable alternative to capitalism. The ultimate failure of the historical attempts at building an attractive alternative to capitalism in the Soviet Union,

China and elsewhere discredited the idea of comprehensive, bureaucratically directed central planning, both because of the highly repressive character of those particular states' processes and because of the pervasive irrationalities produced by these economies. But does this mean that markets must play a central role in any viable alternative to capitalism, or do we need to imagine some entirely new form of planning? Is state ownership of the means of production essential for transcending capitalism, or are a variety of social forms of ownership possible in a postcapitalist economy? Anticapitalists today retain the diagnosis and critique of capitalism, but there is much less clarity about the character of a desirable, viable and achievable alternative that could potentially replace capitalism.

Given all of these ambiguities, perhaps the word "socialism" itself should be dropped. Words accumulate meaning through historical contexts, and maybe socialism has been so compromised by its association with twentieth-century repressive regimes that it can no longer serve well as the umbrella term for emancipatory alternatives to capitalism. Still, in the first decades of the twenty-first century, the idea of socialism has regained some of its positive moral standing. A 2016 Gallup poll indicated that a majority of Americans under thirty had a favorable view of "socialism." And in any case, in much of the world, socialism remains the language for talking about a just and humane alternative to capitalism and no other term has gained wide currency. I will therefore continue to use it here.

This chapter will elaborate a way of thinking about socialism as a potential destination beyond capitalism. In the next section, I will present a particular way of thinking about alternative economic structures. This discussion will involve a foray into fairly abstract social theory, but this is needed in order to give precision to a number of basic concepts. This will be followed by a more concrete discussion of some of the components of a socialist economy that could plausibly realize emancipatory values.

A power-centered concept of socialism

One way to approach rethinking the idea of socialism is to focus on the way power is organized within economic structures, particularly power over the allocation and use of economic resources. Invoking power, of course, opens up a Pandora's box of theoretical issues. Few concepts are more contested by social theorists than power, so here I will adopt a deliberately stripped-down concept: power is the capacity to do things in the world, to produce effects. This is what might be called an "agent-centered" notion of power: people, both acting individually and collectively, use power to accomplish things. In economic systems, they use power to control economic activity—allocating investments, choosing technologies, organizing production, directing work and so on.

Power is the capacity to do things, but there are many different forms this capacity can take. Within economic systems, three different forms of power are particularly salient: economic power, state power and what I will term "social power." The first two of these are familiar. Economic power is based on the control of economic resources. State power is grounded in the control of rulemaking and rule enforcement over a territory. Social power, as I use this expression, is power rooted in the capacity to mobilize people for cooperative, voluntary collective actions. If the exercise of economic power gets people to do things by *bribing* them, and the exercise of state power by *forcing* them, then the exercise of social power gets people to do things by *persuading* them.

Social power is central to the idea of democracy. To say that a state is democratic means that state power is subordinate to social power. The officials in a democratic state, as in all states, wield state power—the power to make and enforce binding rules over territory—but in a political democracy, state power is itself systematically subordinated to social power. The expression "rule by the people" does not really mean "rule by the atomized aggregation of the separate individuals of the society taken as isolated persons," but rather, rule by the people collectively organized into voluntary associations in various ways: parties, communities, unions and so on. Elections are the most familiar way of accomplishing this subordination of state power to social power. The more state power is subordinate to social power, the more profoundly democratic the state.

In terms of these three forms of power, socialism can be distinguished from two other kinds of economic structures, capitalism and statism:

Capitalism is an economic structure within which the allocation and use of resources in the economy is accomplished through the exercise of *economic power*. Investments in and control over production are the result of the exercise of economic power by the owners of capital.

Statism is an economic structure within which the allocation and use of resources for different purposes is accomplished through the exercise of *state power*. State officials control the investment process and production through some sort of state-administrative mechanism, through which they exercise state power.

Socialism is an economic structure within which the allocation and use of resources for different purposes occurs through the exercise of *social power*. In socialism, the investment process and production are controlled through institutions that enable ordinary people to collectively decide what to do. *Fundamentally, this means socialism is equivalent to economic democracy.*

These definitions of capitalism, statism and socialism are what sociologists call "ideal types." As we noted in Chapter 3, actual economies are complex *ecosystems* that vary according to how these different forms of economic relations interact and mix. To call an economy "capitalist" is thus shorthand for a more cumbersome expression like "an economic ecosystem combining capitalist, statist and socialist power relations within which capitalist relations are dominant." In a parallel manner, an economy is statist to the extent that state power is dominant over both economic power and social power. And finally, an economy is socialist to the extent that social power is dominant over state power and economic power.

In this typology of economic forms, there is no mention of markets. This may seem strange since many debates over alternatives to capitalism are framed in terms of markets versus planning. Often, in fact, the very idea of capitalism is equated with markets. This is a mistake. Markets would play a role in any viable statist or socialist economy, as well as in a capitalist economy. The issue is how different forms of power shape the operation of decentralized exchanges within markets, not whether markets exist. Angela Merkel, the chancellor of Germany, is famous for calling for a *market-conforming democracy*; to the contrary, what we need is a *democracy-conforming market*—a market economy that is effectively subordinate to the exercise of democratic power.

The idea of economies as ecosystems combining particular kinds of power relations can be used to describe any unit of analysis—sectors, regional economies, national economies, even the global economy. These power relations also interpenetrate individual units of production, so particular enterprises can be *hybrids* operating in the economic ecosystem that surrounds them. A capitalist firm in which there is a strong workers' council elected by employees and in which representatives of workers sit on the board of directors is a hybrid of capitalist and socialist elements. Such a firm would remain capitalist in that the owners of capital control investments in the firm, but it is a less purely capitalistic firm insofar as control over the firm's operation also involves the exercise of social power.

One of the implications of this way of thinking about economic systems is that the contrast between capitalism and socialism should not be regarded as a simple dichotomy, in which an economy is either one or the other. Instead, we can talk about the *degree* to which an economic system is capitalist or socialist. In these terms, the long-term strategy of eroding capitalism discussed in Chapter 3 envisions a process of expanding and deepening the socialist elements of the economic system in such a way as to undermine the dominance of capitalism. This means deepening and expanding the diverse ways in which economic activities are democratically organized.

Building blocks of a democratic socialist economy

It is one thing to say that the central, organizing idea of socialism is economic democracy. It is quite another to really detail the institutional design of an economy organized around that idea. Traditionally when anticapitalists attempt to do this, they describe some unitary structure of the imagined alternative. Sometimes this takes the form of fine-grain blueprints. More frequently, the alternative is specified in terms of one distinctive institutional mechanism, such as state ownership with central planning, decentralized participatory planning or market socialism with cooperatively owned and managed firms.

I cannot propose such a unitary structure for democratic socialism. I don't think this is just a failure of imagination (although, of course, it may be). Rather, I think a model of a socialist economy revolving around a single institutional mechanism is very unlikely to be viable. The optimal institutional configuration of a democratic-egalitarian economy is much more likely to be a mix of diverse forms of participatory planning, public enterprises, cooperatives, democratically regulated private firms, markets, and other institutional forms, rather than to rely exclusively on any one of these.

In any case, the design of economic institutions in a sustainable postcapitalist democratic economy would evolve through experimentation and democratic deliberation. "Sustainability" in a democratic-egalitarian economy means that the institutional configuration in question would be continually endorsed by the broad majority of participants in the economy, since they have the power to change the rules of the game if they don't like the way things are working. There will inevitably be trade-offs across the different values that a democratic economy hopes to realize; a particular set of institutional rules of the game is a way to navigate those trade-offs. A stable system is one in which the continual long-term results of the system's operation reinforce people's commitment to those rules.

I do not know what institutional configuration of different forms of economic organization would work best, or what, in practice, the trade-offs would be between the possible configurations. But what I do predict is that a stable institutional configuration will contain a heterogeneous set of institutional forms.

Thus, rather than attempt anything approaching a comprehensive blueprint, what follows is a partial inventory of the key building blocks of democratic socialism. Many of these already exist within capitalist economies in various degrees of development, and thus constitute immanent alternatives; others are proposals for new institutional arrangements that could be, but have not yet been, implemented within capitalism, at least in some partial form; and others probably could not be implemented so long as capitalism remains dominant. Taken together, they constitute some of the basic ingredients of a democratic destination beyond capitalism.

Unconditional basic income

Unconditional basic income (UBI) constitutes a fundamental redesign of the mechanisms of income distribution. The idea is quite simple: every legal resident of a territory receives an income sufficient to live above the poverty line without any work requirement or other conditions. Taxes increase to pay for the UBI, so even though everyone gets the income, income earners above a certain threshold would be net contributors (their increase in taxes would be larger than the UBI they receive). Existing public programs of income support would be eliminated, except for those connected to special needs (that is, disabilities requiring extra income). Minimum-wage laws would also be unnecessary, since there would no longer be any reason to prohibit low-wage voluntary contracts once a person's basic needs are not contingent on that wage. The UBI for children would be calibrated at some appropriate level compared to that for adults.

Most defenses of UBI revolve around ways in which a basic income would eliminate poverty, reduce inequality and advance social justice. These are, of course, important issues. If a UBI is reasonably generous, it would constitute a significant step toward the egalitarian ideal of providing everyone with equal access to the material conditions needed to live a flourishing life. However, in the present context, there is an additional important consequence of UBI: in a world with UBI, people can much more easily choose to engage in initiatives to build new forms of economic and social relations. A hallmark of capitalism is that most adults need access to paid employment in order to acquire their necessities of life. While means-tested income-transfer programs of the welfare state have somewhat mitigated this necessity, it is nevertheless difficult for most people to say "no" to the capitalist labor market. UBI makes this much easier and thus opens up an array of new possibilities for people.

For example, in an economic system with UBI, market-oriented worker cooperatives would become much more viable since meeting the basic needs of the worker-owners would not depend on the income generated by the enterprise. This also means worker cooperatives would be better credit risks to banks, making it easier for cooperatives to get loans.

UBI would constitute a massive transfer of resources to the arts, enabling people to opt for a life centered around creative activity rather than market-generated income; and it does so without the heavy administrative controls and priorities of traditional state support of the arts through grants and targeted subsidies, or the biases of elite arts foundations. UBI can also provide livelihood support to small farmers without targeted government agricultural subsidies, which generally benefit agribusiness more than family farms. UBI thus creates a potential alliance of poets and peasants, allowing them to engage in market and nonmarket activities from a base of security rather than vulnerability.

The social and solidarity economy, including new forms of caregiving cooperatives, would be invigorated by an unconditional basic income. UBI would also be a way of supporting people who provide care work for family members outside of the market. Given the demographic pressures of an aging population, UBI can be thought of as a component of an egalitarian, community-based, needs-oriented solution to the problem of caring for the frail aged.

Unconditional basic income can thus be considered one of the core building blocks of a democratic socialist economy, not simply a way of reducing some of the harms of capitalism.

The cooperative market economy

While markets may be an essential feature of any viable complex economy, capitalist firms operating under capitalist rules need not dominate them. A cooperative market economy is one alternative way of organizing market-oriented economic activity that expands the scope for democratic processes. The idea of "cooperatives" includes a very heterogeneous set of economic organizations: consumer cooperatives, owned by consumers and indirectly governed by consumer-members who elect the board of directors; credit cooperatives (typically called credit unions), formally governed by their members; producer cooperatives, whose members are privately owned firms that join together for various purposes, especially food processing, distribution and marketing; housing cooperatives, including communal housing, co-housing and various other forms; solidarity cooperatives, governed by elected boards of stakeholders; and worker cooperatives, owned by workers and governed democratically on a one-person-one-vote basis. All of these are relevant to building a cooperative market economy. In democratic socialism, the rules of the game will be designed to facilitate the vitality of this array of cooperative economic organizations.

Cooperatives enhance economic democracy for two reasons. First, cooperatives are themselves, to varying degrees and in different ways, governed by democratic principles. They are thus constituent elements of a more democratic economy. Second, because cooperatives are geographically rooted, the capital invested in cooperatives is much less mobile and thus unlikely to move to avoid state regulation. While cooperatives, like all market-oriented firms, may oppose certain regulations that impinge on their profits, they are less likely to be able block such regulation through threats to move outside of the jurisdiction of the state. Cooperatives are thus more easily subordinate to democratic priorities formulated through the state.

Taken as a whole, this array of cooperative economic organizations is already a significant element in existing market economies. A 2014 United Nations report on "Measuring the Size and Scope of the Cooperative Economy" indicates that in Europe and North America, over a third of the population holds membership in some kind of cooperative; cooperatives generated over 7 percent of the GDP in Europe and 4 percent in North America. Mostly, however, these are credit unions, consumer cooperatives and producer cooperatives, many of which operate much like ordinary capitalist firms. The form of cooperative that represents the sharpest alternative to capitalist organization, worker cooperatives, tends to be small and plays only a limited role in existing capitalist economies.

Worker cooperatives are particularly salient for the possibility of economic democracy, for in a worker cooperative, workers own the firm and production is governed through democratic processes. While worker cooperatives produce for the market, they are organized around values very different from capitalist firms: solidarity, equality, democratic governance, dignity of work, community development. In capitalist economies, with few exceptions, worker cooperatives tend to be isolated, small firms on the margins of the economy. In a democratic socialist economy, worker cooperatives would potentially constitute a substantial sector, perhaps even the dominant form of organization engaged in market production for many goods and services.

There are reasons to believe that the prospects for worker cooperatives in the twenty-first century may be improving. In particular, technological changes connected to the information technology (IT) revolution have reduced the economies of scale in many sectors of the economy, thus reducing the competitive advantages of large-scale production. This in turn makes worker-owned and democratically governed firms potentially more viable. To use classical Marxist terminology, the changing forces of production expand the possibilities for new relations of production.

That said, unless there are significant changes in the rules of the game within capitalist economies, this potential is unlikely to be realized. Some of the changes in rules that would open up more space for worker cooperatives include:

- *Unconditional basic income.* As noted, UBI would reduce the dependency of worker-owners on market income generated by the cooperative enterprise and thus reduce the risks of forming a cooperative.

- *Public programs to facilitate the conversion of capitalist firms, especially small, family-owned firms, into worker cooperatives.* Programs already exist in the United States and other countries to facilitate capitalist firms distributing shares to employees. While power in such Employee Stock Ownership Programs (ESOPs) remains based on one share, one vote, ESOPs could become a bridge between a capitalist corporation and a fully worker-owned, democratically governed firm.

- *Specialized public credit institutions to support cooperatives.* Since cooperatives are a critical component of an economy oriented to realizing the values of equality, democracy and solidarity, there is a justification for creating public institutions designed to direct resources toward cooperative development. While unconditional basic income will make it easier for worker cooperatives to get loans from ordinary commercial banks, there are still capital needs for cooperative development that would be unmet by purely market-oriented banking. This implies the need for new public credit institutions with a mandate to make loans to cooperatives at below-market rates.

- *Publicly supported cooperative development initiatives.* There is a potentially important role for municipalities in fostering cooperative development. One of the major barriers to cooperatives is access to affordable space, especially in highly urban areas. Cities are in a position to create dedicated space for cooperatives as part of long-term community development projects—in one model, for example, cities own the land and buildings and lease space to cooperatives. Another model envisions space controlled by community trusts and governed by boards elected by cooperatives and other stakeholders.

- *Publicly funded training programs for cooperative organizations and management.* Running a worker cooperative is not a simple matter, especially once a cooperative grows beyond a very small size. Capitalist firms operate in an environment of business schools and management training programs that provide skills needed for their operation. A vibrant cooperative market economy needs educational programs to develop and disseminate the organizational skills needed to manage democratic firms effectively.

These changes in the rules of the game of capitalism would enable worker cooperatives to become a robust part of the cooperative market economy.

The social and solidarity economy

The *social and solidarity economy* is an umbrella term covering a range of economic activities and organizations that are anchored in communities, embody egalitarian and solidaristic values, and are committed to some kind of needs-oriented or social justice mission. Often the organizations within the social/solidarity economy are cooperatives, but they may be other kinds of enterprises: nonprofits, mutual societies, voluntary associations, community organizations, social enterprises (commercial firms with a strong social mission) or even churches. In some parts of the world, the social/solidarity economy overlaps with what is called the "informal economy," economic activity that falls outside of officially recognized and publicly regulated economic activity. But the social/

solidarity economy can also involve durable organizations with permanent staff.

Often the social/solidarity economy emerges in the context of poor and underserved communities as a survival strategy to fill gaps in social provision. When there is a severe economic crisis, as occurred in Argentina in 2000 and Greece in 2009, all sorts of social/solidarity economy activities proliferate: time banking and local currencies; community kitchens; DIY tool libraries; community gardens; caregiving exchanges; free clinics; and much more. However, the social/solidarity economy is not simply a response to marginalization and precariousness; it is also fostered by people trying to build economic relations on a more communitarian, needs-oriented basis. The Canadian province of Quebec, for example, has a vibrant social/solidarity economy that includes daycare centers, eldercare and disability care services, recycling, performing arts, affordable housing projects, makerspaces and a diversity of cooperatives. Activists involved in the social/solidarity economy generally see their work as building emancipatory enclaves within capitalism that enable people to live very different kinds of lives.

The space for the social/solidarity economy would almost certainly expand in a democratic socialist economy. UBI would not only help underwrite market-oriented cooperatives, but also make it easier for people to opt for nonmarket social/solidarity economy activities since the need to generate a livelihood within those activities would be greatly reduced. Furthermore, the social/solidarity economy may constitute the optimal way of providing certain kinds of services. Childcare, eldercare and disability care services are good examples. In principle, these services can be provided through four different kinds of processes: directly by the state, by profit-making market-based firms, by families, or by various kinds of organizations in the social/solidarity economy. In a democratic socialist economy, all four of these options would be available, but the social economy form of care services, underwritten by public funding, would likely be especially vibrant. The public funding embodies the egalitarian value of making the service accessible to all; the social/solidarity economy form of provision enhances the values of community and democratic participation.

Democratizing capitalist firms

The idea of eroding capitalism is not simply a matter of undermining the dominance of capitalist investments and firms in the market; it also involves eroding the capitalist character of capitalist firms themselves. What does this mean? Eroding the capitalist character of firms means restricting the array of rights that accompany "owning the means of production." Property rights in the means of production are actually complex bundles of rights, and over time within capitalist societies, the state has imposed significant constraints on these rights. Minimum-wage laws, for example, restrict the right of employers to pay whatever someone is willing to accept. Health and safety rules regulating the workplace restrict the right to organize the production process in a dangerous manner. Pollution and product safety laws restrict the right to impose costs on others, even if this would be the optimal profit-maximizing strategy of a firm. Employment security laws restrict the ability of employers to fire workers whenever they like. In a democratic socialist economy, these constraints on the private property rights of capitalist firms would be extended and deepened in order to advance the values of equality, democracy and solidarity. Such firms would remain capitalist insofar as individuals can invest their capital in firms and receive a return on their investment, but the rights accorded to firms that accompany such private investment would be much more democratically restricted than in a capitalist economy.

One dimension of capitalist property rights poses a particularly sharp challenge to the idea of economic democracy: the right of employers to organize firms as authoritarian workplaces in which ordinary workers play no systematic role in decision-making. In a capitalist economy, it seems to most people natural that power is concentrated in the hands of the employer, whether the employer is a single person or the top management of a corporation. When you are hired to work in a private firm, of course the employer has the right to tell you what to do, so long as the orders do not violate the law. You can always quit if you don't like the orders. In a democratic socialist economy, the basic rights of democracy would extend into the workplace. This has already occurred in limited ways within some capitalist economies. In Germany, for example, codetermination laws require that workers elect just under half of the board of directors in firms employing more than 2,000 workers, and a third in firms employing 500–2,000 workers. Many countries have rules requiring elected workers' councils in firms over a certain size, which give workers a measure of power over working conditions and conflicts within the workplace.

In a democratic socialist economy, the democratic power of workers within capitalist firms would be extended and deepened. Isabelle Ferreras, in her book *Firms as Political Entities* (Cambridge University Press, 2017), has proposed one way of accomplishing this: All capitalist firms above a certain size would be governed by a bicameral board of directors, one elected by shareholders in a conventional manner and the other elected by workers on a one-person-one-vote basis. She argues that firms are political entities quite analogous to states. The largest global corporations, after all, have annual incomes much larger than most countries. During the development of representative democracy in states, there was frequently a period in which one chamber of a bicameral system represented property owners (such as the House of Lords in Great Britain) and the other chamber represented the people (the House of Commons). In a parallel manner, a bicameral board of directors could choose the top management teams of modern corporations, and all important corporate policy decisions would have to be voted on and passed by both chambers. This would significantly constrain the exercise of economic power within corporations and expand the role for social power.

Banking as a public utility

Further on the need for specialized, public-sector credit institutions in the discussion of cooperatives, more broadly, in a democratic socialist economy, banks would mostly be public utilities rather than private firms maximizing profits for their owners. Most people think of banks as a specialized kind of business that receives savings from people—the depositors—and then lends those savings out to other people and businesses in the form of loans. Banks, in this understanding, are an intermediary between people who want to earn an interest rate on savings and people who have projects for which they need loans. This "loanable funds model" is not, in fact, how banking works. Without going into the technical details, banks lend out vastly more money in loans than they take in through deposits. In effect, they create money when they make new loans. How do they do this? They do it by borrowing money from the central bank at a lower interest than they receive from the loans they issue. And here's the trick: the central bank just creates the money out of nothing. This is important in a market economy because it enables people to launch productive projects without personally having to save enough funds to do so.

This money-creation activity only works because in capitalist economies, states authorize and endorse private profit-making banks to create money—a public function. This makes private banks, as legal scholar Robert Hockett puts it, state franchises. In capitalism, the mandate of banks is to maximize profits for their owners; in a socialist economy, banks would be treated as a public utility and their mandate would include a range of social priorities. More specifically, banks would be authorized to consider the positive social externalities of loans directed toward different kinds of firms and projects.

Would privately owned, profit-oriented banks exist alongside public banks in a democratic socialist economy? Would the economic ecosystem of banking, like the broader ecosystem of the market, include capitalist banks? Like all questions of the detailed configuration of economic forms in a democratic economy, this is an issue that would be resolved through pragmatic experimentation and democratic deliberation. There could well be an appropriate niche for capitalist banking in a socialist economy, but only if the dynamic effects of such banks did not undermine the durability of democratic subordination of economic power.

Nonmarket economic organization

While markets would play a significant role in any viable democratic socialism, it is not the case that a democratically subordinated economy should consist exclusively, or even mainly, of firms producing for markets. Exactly what the balance will ultimately be between market and nonmarket forms of economic activity is something that would evolve over time and be subject to democratic deliberation. One thing, however, is virtually certain: in an economy that was effectively democratized, nonmarket-oriented economic activity in a variety of forms would play a much more important role than in contemporary capitalism.

State provision of goods and services

The most familiar form of nonmarket provision of goods and services connected to the idea of socialism is direct state provision. This need not imply, however, that the form of provision would be through centralized, top-down bureaucracies. The state's responsibility for providing specific goods and services can take the form both of the state directly organizing such production, and of the state funding and overseeing a range of non-state forms of organization. This opens up space for highly decentralized ways of producing state-funded services involving the active participation of local communities and organizations in state–social economy partnerships.

It is not a simple matter, of course, to figure out precisely which services are best produced through markets, or which directly by the state, and which would best be organized through state funding to various kinds of non-state organizations. This is one of things that would be decided through a process of democratic deliberation and experimentation in a democratic socialist economy. But state provision directly and indirectly would certainly include most of the following: caregiving services—health care, childcare, eldercare, disability care; public amenities for community events and processes—community centers, parks and recreation facilities, theaters, art galleries and museums; education at all levels, including continuing education, lifelong learning centers and skill retraining programs; conventional physical infrastructure for transportation; and a range of public utilities. Collectively, these functions could easily encompass well over 50 percent of total economic activity in a technologically advanced capitalist economy.

State provision of these kinds of services is an element of the state-socialist component of capitalist economic systems. In the neoliberal era, significant segments of such state provision have been partially or wholly privatized, often through the state subcontracting the delivery of the service to capitalist corporations. In the United States, this has included the creation of for-profit private prisons that sell prison services and military subcontractors that sell armed security services to the state. Highways in some cases have been sold or leased to private corporations. In Sweden, the iconic social democratic country, for-profit capitalist corporations have been subcontracted to run a significant number of publicly funded schools. Railways have been privatized in many countries, as have water treatment and delivery services.

Some things, of course, could be effectively provided by both the state and markets, and so the issue becomes the mix between the two. Consider access to books. Bookstores and libraries readily provide both. Commercial bookstores distribute books to people on the basis of their ability to pay; libraries distribute books to people on the principle "to each according to need." In a library, if a book is already checked out, the person wanting the book is placed on a waiting list. Books are rationed on the deeply egalitarian principle that a day in every person's life is of equal value. A well-resourced library will then use the length of the waiting list as an indicator of the need to order more copies of a book. Libraries often also distribute other important resources: music, videos, access to computers, tools, toys, meeting rooms and, in some libraries, performance spaces. Libraries thus constitute a mechanism of distribution that embodies the egalitarian ideal of giving everyone equal access to the resources needed for a flourishing life. In a democratic socialist economy, there would be an expansion of nonmarket, library-like ways of giving people access to many resources.

When capitalist firms produce services, the market determines the price at which they are sold; when those services are provided by the state, the price consumers are charged becomes a political decision. For some services, it is uncontroversial that they should be free to those who directly use the service: public education is the prime example. But for many forms of state provision, there are ambiguities. Should people be charged entry fees for parks, zoos and museums? What about libraries? Should highways have tolls? A particularly salient example, given environmental considerations, is public transportation. In most places within capitalist societies, even when public transportation is directly provided by the state, riders must buy tickets. In a democratic socialist economy, most public transportation would almost certainly be free for riders. The reason is straightforward: there are very strong positive benefits to the society as a whole, especially for the environment, from high-quality, heavily used public transportation. These positive benefits are what economists call "positive externalities." These positive externalities constitute real value for the society, and if this value were factored into the price of tickets for individual rides, then the optimal price would almost certainly be zero. Because of such positive externalities, in a democratic socialist economy, many publicly funded services are likely to be made available to people without user fees.

Peer-to-peer collaborative production

State provision is by no means the only important form of nonmarket production. In the Internet age, a particularly striking form of nonmarket economic activity is peer-to-peer collaborative production (P2P production). Wikipedia is the most familiar example, involving several hundred thousand people around the world who spend varying amounts of time adding new material, monitoring entries, correcting mistakes and challenging claims in articles. Anyone can edit the contribution of anyone else. None of the contributors are paid. As of 2018, Wikipedia had over 5 million articles in English, and over 1 million articles in thirteen other languages. Moreover, Wikipedia is free to anyone in the world with access to the Internet. Given the increasing role of public libraries in providing computers with Internet access, this means that in all economically developed countries and many less developed countries as well, virtually the entire population has unlimited free access to this resource. Wikipedia was launched in 2001 and virtually destroyed a more than 200-year-old capitalist market in encyclopedias.

Wikipedia exists in a capitalist world, and yet it represents a fundamentally anticapitalist way of both producing and distributing something of considerable value to people. Peer-to-peer collaborative production is not simply *non*capitalist; it is based on values fundamentally opposed to capitalism, especially the values of equality and community. To be sure, in existing capitalist economies, P2P collaborative production occupies a niche alongside capitalist production, and it often interacts smoothly with capitalist firms. For example, the computer operating system Linux was produced and is continually improved through a P2P collaborative process, and yet is used by Google and other high-tech capitalist firms. Those firms see this resource as sufficiently valuable that they are willing to pay some of their software engineers to contribute to the P2P production process even though the firm cannot patent the resulting software. (Linux is patented under an "open-source" license designed to prevent it being turned into private property.) Peer-to-peer collaborative production, just like public libraries, thus simultaneously represents an egalitarian alternative to capitalist relations of production and can be functional for capitalism.

In a democratic socialist economy, P2P collaborative production could play a significant role in facilitating a wide range of economic activities. Consider the following: increasingly in the twenty-first century, significant segments of manufacturing will revolve around computer-driven forms of automated production using things like 3-D printers and automated machine tools. In many contexts, such machines will significantly reduce the economies of scale, thus enabling small-scale producers, organized in cooperatives, to manufacture products on a made-to-order basis. A key issue for such decentralized, IT-enabled small-scale production is how people get access to the design code for the products they wish to produce and the capital equipment. One way of creating and distributing such design code is through P2P networks that create large, globally accessible libraries of free downloadable designs. These designs would be nonproprietary and freely sharable, usable by anyone with access to the necessary means of production. The property rights in the means of production themselves—the numerically controlled machines, 3-D printers and the like—could be organized in a variety of ways: by individual cooperatives; by consortia of cooperatives and small firms; by municipalities or other public bodies and then leased to cooperatives. Peer-to-peer collaborative production of design libraries, then, would solve the problem of generating sophisticated designs for products; creative commons licenses for those designs would solve the problem of equal access; and various forms of public and cooperative ownership would solve the problem of access to the means of production to use those designs.

The knowledge commons

One of the foundations of contemporary capitalist production is intellectual property rights, especially patents. Patents are generally defended on the grounds that they provide necessary incentives for innovation and thus have a positive effect on the rate of innovation. Innovation involves risks, since there is never a guarantee that the time, resources and energy devoted to research and development will actually result in a successful innovation. Many potential innovators would not take those risks unless they had assurance of being able to restrict the access of other people to their innovations. This is the sense in which the promise of a patent acts as an incentive for innovation. But, clearly, patents also have negative effects on the rate of innovation by slowing down the rate of diffusion, copying and improving existing innovations.

It is impossible to know whether on balance the positive effects of intellectual property rights on the incentive for innovation are greater or smaller than the negative effects. What we do know for sure is that patents enable corporations to restrict access to innovation in ways that significantly enhance their profits. This has had particularly grotesque effects in the pharmaceutical industry, where the enforcement of patent protection has enabled corporations to raise the prices of critical drugs vastly above their costs of production, but such "monopoly rents" (to use the economists' expression) occur whenever a valuable patent blocks access to a technology.

In recent decades, activists interested in making knowledge universally available for human purposes have created a number of alternatives to private intellectual property rights. Broadly, these are called "open-access" licenses, and include such things as Copyleft, Patentleft, Creative Commons licenses, and BiOS (Biological Open Source) licenses. These and other licenses have been used to protect the accessible status of open-source software, scientific discoveries with applications to agriculture and medicine, cultural products and other forms of knowledge. In a democratic socialist economy, while there may be a residual role for private intellectual property rights and limited patents, in general scientific and technical knowledge and information would be treated as part of a knowledge commons.

If all of the items on the menu we have been exploring were in place in a substantial way, we would no longer be living in a capitalist economy. The precise mix of different elements and how they would be connected, however, could vary enormously. One can easily imagine a democratic socialist economy within which the direct state provision of many services had been replaced by public funding with social/solidarity economy provision, but equally one in which this was not a prominent part of the economic ecosystem. Democratic socialist economies could vary in the relative scope of market production versus the various forms of nonmarket production of goods and services, or the relative weight of cooperatives versus other forms of market-oriented enterprises. Unconditional basic income could be a pivotal mechanism of income redistribution, but one could also imagine a configuration in which "good jobs for all" was the basic way of guaranteeing livelihoods for everyone able to work, and generous needs-based income transfer programs provided livelihoods for those unable to do so. The various forms of economic organization discussed in this chapter are thus just an inventory of building blocks—and a partial inventory at that. The actual configuration of elements in any future sustainable democratic socialist economy beyond capitalism would be the result of an extended process of democratic experimentation over time.

Back to the problem of strategy

Given this conception of a destination beyond capitalism, the fundamental strategic problem we face is how to create the conditions in which such sustained democratic experimentalism is possible. So long as capitalism remains dominant, such experimentation is deeply constrained. The strategic vision elaborated in Chapter 3 argues, however, that it might be possible to gradually create such conditions by eroding the dominance of capitalism through a combination of dismantling and taming capitalism from above and resisting and escaping capitalism from below.

Given how constraining capitalist relations are on the project of democratizing the economy, it is easy to see the appeal of the classic revolutionary idea that the dominance of capitalism can only be broken by a rupture in the power relations that sustain that dominance. This seizure of power would then set in motion the long-term project in which democratic experimentation could function to build the emancipatory alternative. I argued that this ruptural vision is a fantasy, at least for the foreseeable future, since it is not plausible that a system rupture could set in motion the sustained democratic experimentation needed to build a democratic, egalitarian, solidaristic economy. To be sure, it is certainly possible that a system rupture might occur in the future in a situation of intense crisis; however, there is evidence that this would not create the conditions for democratic socialism.

But, isn't eroding the dominance of capitalism equally implausible? It is one thing to argue that there is space within capitalism for resisting the depredations of capitalism. This happens all the time. And escaping capitalism, in the sense of building economic relations embodying emancipatory values in cracks and niches, is also possible; just consider cooperatives, peer-to-peer production, the social economy and public libraries. These are all possible "moves in the game" even when capitalism is dominant. The problem is that capitalism's rules of the game severely restrict the space for such moves. Specifically, the existing rules seem unlikely to allow alternatives to grow in ways that would significantly erode capitalism's dominance. This is why the strategy of eroding capitalism also requires *dismantling* capitalism—that is, changing the rules of the game that make up the power relations of capitalism in such a way as to open up more space for emancipatory alternatives. Historically, capitalism's rules have sometimes been altered to neutralize some of its worst harms. This is taming capitalism. Dismantling it goes beyond simply neutralizing harms; it involves changes in those rules of the game that impinge on the core power relations of capitalism. This is a much bigger challenge.

To understand the nature of this challenge, we must turn our attention to the state. This is the focus of the next chapter.

5

Anticapitalism and the State

Many people who share the emancipatory aspirations for a more egalitarian, democratic and solidaristic world are nevertheless very skeptical of the strategy of eroding capitalism. At the center of this skepticism is the belief that the character of the state in capitalist societies makes this impossible. The strategy of eroding capitalism combines initiatives within civil society to build emancipatory economic alternatives in the spaces where this is possible, with interventions from the state to expand those spaces in various ways. Thus, while the strategy is not simply state-directed from above, it does require at least partial support from the state. Skeptics naturally ask: if emancipatory forms of economic activities and relations ever grew to the point of threatening the dominance of capitalism, wouldn't they simply be crushed by the state? And if anticapitalist political forces managed democratically to gain control of the state in order to push forward an anticapitalist agenda, wouldn't this simply provoke the destruction of democracy itself by pro-capitalist forces? Consider what happened in Chile in 1973 when the democratically elected Allende government pursued a socialist agenda: the government was overthrown in a military coup followed by seventeen years of repressive dictatorship. So, how can eroding capitalism constitute an effective strategy for transcending it, given the class character and coercive power of the state?

To address this question, we have to grapple with some difficult issues in the theory of the state.

The problem of the capitalist state

The key issue is the extent to which states in capitalist societies are coherent, integrated, effective machines for ensuring the long-term dominance of capitalism.

There is a long tradition in theoretical discussions by critics of capitalism that sees the state in capitalist society as designed to reproduce capitalism. Two interconnected arguments animate this claim: First, the state is controlled by powerful elites deeply linked to the capitalist class. They wield state power broadly to serve the interests of that class and, above all, block any serious challenges to capitalism. Second, the institutional design of the very machinery of the state contributes to reproducing capitalism. The idea here is not simply that the state is used by powerful elites to serve their interests—although, to be sure, that may be true as well—but that the inner structure of the state has built-in biases in favor of the interests of the capitalist class. For this reason, this kind of state is called a *capitalist state* rather than simply a *state in capitalist society*. These two arguments reinforce each other: The first argument explains why the people who make decisions in the state are generally hostile to anticapitalist projects; the second argument explains why, even when it happens that political actors with genuine anticapitalist objectives get into positions of power, they are unable to sustainably pursue anticapitalist policies. Together, these arguments imply that the capitalist state cannot serve as a political instrument for maintaining a strategy of eroding the dominance of capitalism.

Here are a few examples that are often cited as features of the capitalist state that contribute to the reproduction of capitalism:

- The capitalist state obtains its revenues from taxing income generated in the capitalist market economy. This means that the state is dependent on a vibrant, healthy, profitable capitalism: without profits, there is no investment; if private investment declines, income and jobs decline; if income and jobs decline, taxes decline. State actions that undermine capitalist profits, therefore, ultimately harm the state itself. Even left-wing political forces, whenever they are in power, must worry about a "good business climate."
- The mechanisms for the recruitment of powerful state officials—both politicians and bureaucratic officials—systematically favor elites over ordinary citizens. This creates strong biases in favor of preserving inequalities of power and privilege, both because of the specific interests of those who wield political power and because of the ways political elites are embedded in social networks that tie them to capitalist elites. Even if a political party opposed to capitalism wins elections, it will face a bureaucratic structure filled with people hostile to anticapitalism.
- The sanctity of private property rights inscribed in the "rule of law," combined with the procedural rules that govern courts, insure that capitalist property is strongly protected by the capitalist state.

In the strongest versions of this theory of the capitalist state, these and other structural features of the state insure that its central function is to defend and reproduce capitalism. In weaker versions, these features do not *guarantee* that the capitalist state will be functional for capitalism—states may do all sorts of stupid things that harm capitalism. Nevertheless, the capitalist character of the state obstructs the possibility of the state engaging systematically in policies that go against capitalism. Sustained *anticapitalism* is blocked by the nature of the capitalist state even if not everything the state does is optimal for capitalism.

The theory captures an important reality: existing states in capitalist societies have biases that are hardwired into their structure, and these biases broadly serve to support capitalism. But this does not mean that the state, in spite of these structural biases, cannot potentially be used to undermine the dominance of capitalism as well. Two issues are especially important to consider: First, the apparatuses that make up the state are filled with internal contradictions; and second, the functional demands on the state are contradictory. Let's look at each of these in turn.

Internal contradictions of the state

A pivotal claim in our discussion of eroding capitalism in Chapter 3 and of democratic socialism as a destination beyond capitalism in Chapter 4 was that the concept of "capitalism" should be treated as an ideal type; actual economic systems are messy combinations of capitalist and noncapitalist relations, and some of these noncapitalist relations may even be anticapitalist. This is why we described capitalism as an economic ecosystem within which capitalism is dominant rather than exclusively present.

The same idea should be applied to the state. The concept of the "capitalist state" is also an ideal type. Actual capitalist states consist of loosely coupled, heterogeneous systems of apparatuses, within which the mechanisms that help reproduce capitalism are dominant. State apparatuses, like economic ones, embody pro-capitalist biases to varying and uneven degrees across time and between places. This variation in the balance of class and other interests embodied in different parts of the state is the result of the specific history of struggles over the state. The trajectory of compromises and concessions, victories and defeats, is thus registered in both the formal design and informal norms within political institutions.

Of particular relevance in the variability in the capitalist character of different state apparatuses is the problem of democracy. The more robustly democratic the forms of decision-making and accountability, the less purely capitalist the class character of a state apparatus. Even ordinary parliamentary democracy has always had a contradictory class character: while it may be true that the rules of the game of electoral democracy have the general effect of constraining and taming class struggles over the state in ways that support capitalist dominance, it is also true that to the extent elections involve real democratic competition, they introduce potential tensions and uncertainties in the class character of legislative bodies. In times of crisis and popular mobilization, those tensions can loosen the limits of possibility for new forms of state initiatives.

Struggles to deepen and revitalize democracy can thus be thought of as potentially diluting—not eliminating, but diluting—the capitalist character of state apparatuses. This is not simply a question of enhancing the democratic processes of ordinary state machinery, but also of the wide variety of commissions and organizations that interface with all modern states. Deepening democracy is also not simply a question of the democratization of centralized national states, but of local and regional state apparatuses as well. Struggles over the democratic quality of the local state may be especially important in terms of thinking about ways in which state initiatives can enlarge the space for noncapitalist economic initiatives.

Contradictory, contested functionality

As mentioned, capitalism is filled with self-destructive tendencies. Familiar examples include:

- Each employer wants to pay employees as little as possible in order to maximize profits, but this then depresses the buying power of consumers in the market, which in turn makes it harder to sell the things capitalists produce.
- If a firm provides good on-the-job training it will have more productive workers, but providing this training is expensive. If some firms in a sector provide this training and others do not, then the firms that provide the training risk having their workers poached by competitors who didn't have to bear the costs of training. The result is that all firms are hesitant to make extensive on-the-job training investments.
- Financial sectors are prone to speculative "bubbles" in which people borrow money to invest in assets whose price is rising. Investors figure that they can repay the loans easily when they sell the asset because asset prices are going up. As more people borrow money to invest in the asset, this pushes the asset price even higher. Eventually the bubble bursts and the price collapses, which means that many investors default on their loans, which in turn triggers a crisis in the banking sector. The result is

periodic serious economic crises that destroy many firms, create great harm to large numbers of people, and increase social instability.

- The inequalities in wealth and income generated by capitalism tend to increase over time; this creates conflicts, especially class conflicts, which can become very costly to contain.

- Firms have strong incentives to displace costs onto others when they can get away with it, the classic example being pollution. Over time, such negative externalities can degrade the environment in ways that are costly for everyone. The climate crisis is the most striking example.

- Capitalist competition among firms generates winners and losers, which cumulatively tends to concentrate power within particular sectors. Such monopoly power enables firms to act in predatory ways, both toward consumers and toward other capitalist firms.

If capitalism were left to its own devices, these and other self-destructive tendencies would undermine the viability of capitalism itself. The idea that the capitalist state serves the function of reproducing capitalism means that the state has the responsibility of providing various kinds of regulations and interventions—steering mechanisms, some call them—to counteract these self-destructive processes.

This turns out to be a difficult task for several reasons: Often the complexity of the problems means that it is far from obvious what sorts of policies are optimal for reproducing capitalism; effective solutions to a given problem may involve going against the interests of particular sectors or groups of capitalists, and their resistance may be sufficient to block functional solutions; the multiplicity of the different conditions for reproducing capitalism means that a solution to some of these destructive tendencies may undermine solutions to others. This last issue may be the most vexing. For example, state policies to reduce social conflicts of various sorts through the development of the welfare state may, over time, require levels of taxation and redistribution that encroach on capital accumulation. This is sometimes referred as the contradiction between the legitimation function of the state (fostering consent and thus reducing conflict) and the accumulation function of the state (creating optimal conditions for profits and capital accumulation). Another example is state policies that support labor unions. Such policies can be functional for capitalism in so far as they help to dampen disruptive class conflict and foster constructive collaboration between managers and workers within firms, but over time strong labor unions can introduce rigidities in employment that make it more difficult for firms to respond to competitive challenges internationally. The complexity and multidimensionality of the functional requirements for reproducing capitalism means that there may never be a stable equilibrium: over time, solutions to some problems only intensify others.

Underlying many of these contradictions in the efforts of the capitalist state to support capitalism is what can be described as temporal inconsistencies between the relatively short-term effects of state actions for supporting capitalism and the long-run dynamic consequences. State actions concerned with supporting dominant economic structures are mainly responses to immediate conditions, challenges and pressures. But responses to these challenges may have quite different long-term effects. There is thus often a disjuncture between effective short-term state actions and the longer-term dynamic ramifications of those actions, which sometimes can become real threats to the existing structures of power. As noted in Chapter 3, this is one way of understanding the erosion of feudalism. The feudal state facilitated merchant capitalism in various ways even though in the long run, the dynamics of merchant capitalism corroded feudal relations. Merchant capitalism helped solve immediate problems for the feudal ruling class, and this is what mattered.

Similarly, in the middle of the twentieth century, the capitalist state facilitated the growth of a vibrant public sector and public regulation of capitalism associated with social democracy. Social democracy helped solve a series of problems within capitalism commonly referred to as "market failures": insufficient aggregate demand to provide robust markets for capitalist production; destructive volatility in financial markets; inadequate public goods to provide for the stable reproduction of labor; and so on. In helping to solve these problems, social democracy strengthened capitalism—but, crucially, it did so while it expanded the space for various socialist elements in the economic ecosystem: the partial decommodification of labor power through state provision of significant components of workers' material conditions of life; the increase in working-class social power within capitalist firms and the labor market through favorable labor laws; and the deepening of the administrative capacity of the state to impose effective capital regulation to deal with the most serious negative externalities of investors' and firms' behavior in capitalist markets (pollution, product and workplace hazards, predatory market behavior, market volatility and other issues). The short-run, practical solutions embodied principles that had the potential in the long term to weaken capitalism's dominance. Many capitalists may not have embraced these state initiatives and even felt threatened by them, but the social democratic state did help solve practical problems and therefore was tolerated.

The fact that this array of state actions contributed to the stability of mid-twentieth century capitalism is sometimes taken as an indication that there was nothing noncapitalist about these policies, and certainly that they could not in any way be considered corrosive of capitalism. This is a mistake. It is entirely possible for a form of state intervention to have the immediate effect of solving problems for capitalism, and even strengthening it, and nevertheless set in motion dynamics that have the potential to erode the dominance of capitalism over time. This is why in the United States, the right wing always called the New Deal "creeping socialism." Indeed, it is precisely the tendency of social democratic initiatives to expand in ways that encroach on capitalism that eventually lead to the attacks on the social democratic state under the banner of neoliberalism. As capitalists and their political allies came increasingly to see the expansive state as creating progressively suboptimal conditions for capital accumulation, they waited for the political opportunity to launch an offensive against the affirmative state.

Neoliberalism may have been fairly successful in dismantling, to varying degrees, the socialist elements within the late twentieth-century capitalist state and the capitalist economy in most capitalist societies, but it certainly has not been able to eliminate the contradictory pressures on the state or the internal contradictions in its political structures. In the first decades of the twenty-first century, these contradictions have become acute, generating a pervasive sense of crisis within both the economy and the state. This in turn opens up the state for new initiatives that solve immediate problems in ways that potentially create spaces for the expansion of noncapitalist alternatives.

Prospects

Gramsci is famous for saying that we need pessimism of the intellect but optimism of the will. But we also need at least a little optimism of the intellect to sustain the optimism of the will. There are two trends that suggest some grounds for optimism about future possibilities for the kinds of state initiatives that could potentially unleash dynamics of long-term erosion of capitalist dominance.

First, global warming is likely to spell the end of neoliberalism as a specific form of capitalism. Even aside from the issue of mitigating climate change through a conversion to non-carbon emitting energy production, the necessary adaptations to global warming will require a massive expansion of state-provided public goods. The market is simply not going to build sea walls to protect Manhattan. The scale of resources needed for such state interventions could easily reach the levels of the major wars of the twentieth century. Even though capitalist firms will profit enormously from the production of such infrastructural public goods—just as they profit from military production in times of war—substantial tax increases and state planning will be needed for such an expansive role of the state in the provision of environmental public goods. While neoliberalism has been compatible with high levels of military spending and planning, the shift of state intervention toward large-scale environmental infrastructure and regulations is likely to undermine neoliberalism ideologically and politically. If these processes occur within the framework of capitalist democracy—a big "if," to be sure —then this reinvigoration of the public goods role of the state will open up more political space for a broader array of progressive state actions.

The second trend with which the capitalist state will

have to contend in the course of the twenty-first century is the long-term employment effects from the technological changes of the information revolution. Of course, with every wave of technological change there is speculation that the destruction of jobs by the new technology will lead to widespread marginalization and permanent structural unemployment, but in previous waves, economic growth eventually created sufficient jobs in new sectors to overcome deficits in employment. The forms of automation in the digital age, which are now penetrating deep into the service sector, including sectors of professional services, makes it much less likely that future economic growth will provide adequate employment opportunities through the capitalist market. The magnitude of this problem is further intensified by the globalization of capitalist production. As the twenty-first century progresses, these problems will only get worse and will not be solved by the spontaneous operation of market forces. The result will be increasing precariousness and marginalization of a significant portion of the population. Even aside from social justice considerations, this trend is likely to generate social instability and costly conflict.

These two trends taken together pose major new challenges to the capitalist state: the need for a massive increase in the provision of public goods to deal with climate change, and the need for new policies to deal with broad economic dislocation and insecurity caused by technological change, especially automation and artificial intelligence. One possible trajectory into the future, of course, is that the combination of these challenges leads to an accelerated erosion of democracy within capitalist societies. We already observe this tendency in the United States, with the suppression of voting rights for poor and minority citizens, intensified gerrymandering of electoral districts to favor right-wing political forces and the unfettered role of money in elections. Particularly given the possibility of militarism as a response to the global disruptions of climate change, an authoritarian state with only a veneer of democracy is certainly one scenario. But there is another possible trajectory: a revitalization of democracy within which progressive popular mobilizations have greater political influence. This would open up the possibility of producing new forms of state intervention that could underwrite the expansion of more democratic-egalitarian forms of economic activity coexisting alongside capitalism within the hybrid economic ecosystem.

More specifically, consider the following scenario.

The necessity to deal with adaptations to climate change marks the end of neoliberalism and its ideological strictures. The state embarks on the needed large-scale public works projects and also takes a more intrusive role in economic planning around energy production and transportation systems to accelerate the shift from the carbon-based energy system. In this context, the broader range of roles for the state is back on the political agenda, including an expansive understanding of the need for public goods and the state's responsibility for counteracting increasing marginalization and economic inequality, since full employment through capitalist labor markets seems increasingly implausible.

Two responses by the state to these pressures could significantly increase the democratic socialist elements within the hybrid capitalist economic ecosystem. First, these ideological shifts and political pressures could foster the expansion of state-funded employment in the provision of public goods and services. Wealthy countries can certainly afford such an expansion; the issue is the political willingness to raise taxes for this purpose, not the economic constraints on doing so. Second, the state could take seriously the possibility of more fundamentally changing the connection between livelihoods and jobs through the introduction of UBI, a policy proposal that is already being given increased public discussion in the second decade of the twenty-first century.

Unconditional basic income is a possible form of state intervention that responds to the decline of adequate employment opportunities within capitalist markets while also expanding the potential space for social power within the economy. From the point of view of reproducing capitalism, UBI would accomplish three things. First, it would mitigate the worst effects of inequality and poverty generated by marginalization, and thus contribute to social stability. Second, it would underwrite a different model of income-generating work: the self-creation of jobs to generate discretionary income for people. UBI would make a wide range of market-oriented self-employment opportunities attractive to people even if the self-created jobs did not generate a livable income. One can imagine, for example, that more people would be interested in being small farmers and commercial gardeners if they had a UBI to cover their basic costs of living. Such income would also make participation in the "gig economy" more viable for many people. And third, UBI would stabilize the consumer market for capitalist production. As a system of production, automation in capitalist firms inherently faces the problem of not employing enough people in the aggregate to buy the things produced. UBI provides a widely dispersed demand for basic consumption goods. For these reasons, unconditional basic income may become an attractive policy option for capitalist elites, especially in the context of the exhaustion of neoliberalism as an ideology in the face of a rehabilitated activist regulatory state.

If UBI is an attractive solution to problems facing capitalism, how can it also contribute to the erosion of capitalism? A central feature of capitalism is what Marx referred to as the double separation of workers—their simultaneous separation from the means of production and from the means of subsistence. Unconditional basic income reunites workers with the means of subsistence, even though they remain separated from the means of production; it thus directly modifies the basic class relations of capitalism. As discussed in Chapter 4, a tax-financed UBI provided by the state would enable workers to refuse capitalist employment and choose, instead, to engage in all sorts of noncapitalist economic activities, including those constructed through social power—the social and solidarity economy, worker cooperatives, noncommercial performing arts, community activism and much more. Unconditional basic income thus expands the space for sustainable socialist—i.e., socially empowered—economic relations. All of these possibilities may be further enhanced by the same technological developments that have created the problem of marginalization, since IT broadly reduces economies of scale of production.

The combination of a UBI (to facilitate the exit of people from the capitalist sector of the economy), new technologies (to facilitate the development of noncapitalist forms of production) and a congenial local state to provide better infrastructure for these initiatives means that, over time, the sector of the economy organized through social power could develop deeper roots and expand in as yet unforeseen ways.

All of this would occur, it is important to stress, within capitalism, and thus inevitably these noncapitalist forms of production would have to find ways of positively articulating their opposition to the imperatives of capitalism.

Many inputs to the noncapitalist sector would be themselves produced by capitalist firms; producers in the noncapitalist sector would purchase a significant part of their consumption from capitalist firms; and the state's production of public goods would also often involve contracts with capitalist firms. UBI facilitates exit from capitalist relations, but it also in a sense subsidizes precarious work for capitalist corporations, most notably in the gig economy. Even after this new configuration stabilized, the state would still be superintending an economy within which capitalism remained prominent, and almost certainly dominant. But the dominance of capitalism would be reduced insofar as it would impose much weaker constraints on the ways people gain their livelihoods. This opens new possibilities for ongoing struggles to enlarge the scope of social power within the economy.

In Chapter 3, I referred to reforms that have this double character—both strengthening capitalism by solving problems and expanding the possibilities for building emancipatory alternatives—as *symbiotic* transformations. Often anticapitalists are deeply suspicious of such actions by the state. If UBI ends up subsidizing low-wage jobs in the gig economy, then isn't this a bad thing? Doesn't this mean that the reform has been co-opted by capitalism? This, however, is precisely what makes this kind of reform sustainable. A reform that directly undermined capitalism by promoting anticapitalist alternatives without providing any positive benefits for capitalism would be perpetually vulnerable to being dismantled whenever the political strength of progressive forces declined.

Unconditional basic income thus has a paradoxical relationship to capitalism. On one hand, it can help solve a range of real problems within capitalism and contribute to the vitality of capital accumulation, at least in some sectors.

On the other hand, it has the potential to help unleash a dynamic that expands the space for democratic-egalitarian interstitial transformations in ways that reduce the dominance of capitalism and point the economic ecosystem on a trajectory beyond capitalism. If, then, a generous UBI can be implemented and defended, it could both erode the dominance of capitalism within the overall economic system and strengthen conditions for capital accumulation within the reduced spaces where capitalism operates.

If the limits of possibility inscribed in the capitalist character of the state are so narrow as to prevent state actions that might facilitate the growth of these kinds of noncapitalist economic processes, then the prospects of eroding capitalism are remote. But if there are significant disjunctures between present problem-solving and future consequences, and if popular social forces mobilize around a political agenda of consolidating alternative economic spaces, then a significant expansion of economic activity embodying democratic, egalitarian and solidaristic values could be possible. And this, in turn, could provide the foundation for a potential trajectory beyond capitalism.

Democratizing the state

The capitalist state is not well designed for emancipatory social transformation; it is systematically biased to support the dominance of capitalism, both because of privileged access by corporations and the wealthy to state bureaucracy and because of its institutional structure. But it is also not a perfect machine for reproducing capitalism's dominance. The trick for socialist political forces is to exploit the state's internal inconsistencies as well as the contradictions it faces in solving the problems that capitalism itself creates; taking this action will expand possibilities for creating democratic, egalitarian, solidaristic economic alternatives. Crucial in this prospective change is the quality of democracy within the capitalist state: the more deeply democratic the capitalist state, the greater the possibility of state policies supporting the conditions for noncapitalist alternatives. Struggles to "democratize democracy"—to use the expression of Portuguese sociologist Boaventura Santos—are thus pivotal to eroding capitalism.

Democratizing democracy requires both reversing the antidemocratic effects of neoliberalism on the state and deepening democracy through institutional innovations.

Neoliberalism has undermined democracy in four principal ways: First, reducing the constraints on the global movement of capital has increased the external pressures on states to be attentive to the interests of capital. Second, deregulating the financial sector has increased the power of finance to constrain state policy. Third, privatizing a range of state services has undermined the effective capacity of the state to democratically govern the quality and character of many public services. And finally, weakening the labor movement has undermined the most important sources of working-class associational power in the political arena, not simply within the labor market. One of the conditions for a more democratic capitalist democracy is to reverse these trends: reintroduce sufficient controls on the global movement of capital to give states more maneuverability over economic priorities; reregulate the financial sector in ways that reduce the intensive financialization of the economy; restore direct state involvement in the provision of privatized public services; and create a more favorable legal environment for labor organizing.

Simply undoing neoliberalism's damage to democracy, however, is not enough. The era before neoliberalism should not be treated nostalgically as a golden age of robust democracy. Democracy before neoliberalism was constrained and incomplete in all capitalist states. To make the capitalist state a more congenial setting for fostering the democratization of the economy, it is also necessary to deepen democracy wherever possible. Some of the critical factors here include: democratically empowered decentralization, new forms of citizen participation, new institutions for political representation and democratizing electoral rules of the game.

Democratically empowered decentralization

The idea of decentralizing the state has an ambiguous relationship to democratization. One hallmark of neoliberalism, in fact, has been calls for decentralization, on the grounds that centralized political authority is overly bureaucratic, economically inefficient and often corrupt. Typically, however, neoliberal decentralization is a cover for privatization, marketization and reductions in state spending. Democratically empowered decentralization, in contrast, rests on the idea that for many issues, problem-solving can be more effective when real decision-making power is given to democratic public authorities located closer to the problems. Of particular importance is giving more jurisdiction, autonomy and necessary resources to cities, regions and other decentralized subunits of national states; since meaningful popular participation is also much easier at smaller scales of government, this likewise opens the possibility of vigorous democratic experimentalism with high levels of citizen involvement.

New forms of citizen participation

The decentralization of political power is certainly not enough to enhance democracy. Local levels of government can be corrupt and authoritarian, run by political machines organized around patronage. What we need is a combination of deepening democracy within decentralized levels of government, along with giving such units the necessary power and resources to do things.

One innovative institutional design for accomplishing this is participatory budgeting (PB). In a participatory budget, all or part of an organization's budget is allocated through a process of direct participatory decision-making by the organization's members. PB can be applied to cities, schools, public housing units or any organization that has at least some control over its own budget allocations. The idea originated in the city of Porto Alegre in the early 1990s and from there has spread around the world.

There are many different institutional designs for PB in cities. In New York City, for example, each city council district is allocated a discretionary budget controlled by the elected city councilmember from that district to be used for various kinds of infrastructure projects, from filling street potholes to improvements in parks. The councilmember can thus have the district's residents decide how these discretionary funds are to be used. The amounts allocated in council district PBs vary, but they are generally in the $1–2 million range per year. Residents of the district then volunteer for committees to develop project proposals to use the funds. After the city government's technical staff determines each proposal's costs, residents in the district then can vote on their preferences for implementing the projects. In the New York City case, teenagers and undocumented immigrants could fully participate in both the project development and voting processes.

Participatory budgeting in one form or another now exists in hundreds of cities around the world. Sometimes the powers of a PB are quite marginal, providing recommendations to the city government but not actually controlling part of the budget. Sometimes a PB process becomes another way for politicians to distribute favors, becoming a new kind of patronage machine rather than an expression of democratic participation. And almost everywhere, the amount of funding directly controlled through participatory budgeting is relatively small. Nevertheless, the institutional principles of participatory budgeting and other forms of direct democracy at the local level have the potential to become a significant way of deepening democracy by enhancing the possibility of empowered popular participation.

New institutions for democratic representation

Participatory budgeting is only one of a variety of innovative institutional devices that are being experimented with to enhance meaningful democratic participation. Another innovation for deepening democracy involves the random selection of citizens to participate in certain kinds of decision-making bodies. The most familiar example of this is a jury, in which randomly selected citizens decide on the outcome of court proceedings. Random selection has also been used in consultative bodies—sometimes called "mini publics"—in order provide input into the decisions of various kinds of government agencies and departments. A more far-reaching proposal is to replace, within a two-chamber legislative system, one of the elected chambers with a chamber filled through random selection. There are, of course, many details to fine-tune for this to be workable, but the basic idea is that a legislative chamber of randomly selected ordinary citizens would more accurately reflect the demographic composition of the population than is the case in elected legislatures, which are invariably filled by relatively privileged people.

A random assembly would be in a better position to deliberate over issues in ways that reflect the spectrum of interests in the society and seek compromises in ways that are less dominated by elite interests.

Democratizing electoral rules of the game

While novel forms of empowered citizen participation could contribute to a more robustly democratic society, it is almost certainly the case that any viable democratic system will continue to rely heavily on elections to choose a range of political officials. A central problem for democratizing democracy, therefore, revolves around the problem of how to make electoral democracy more robustly democratic.

The specific problems with existing electoral rules vary from place to place. The kind of electoral system used in the United States is especially flawed because of the ways single-member districts are prone to gerrymandering. But every system, even those with reasonable mechanisms of proportional representation, operates in ways that violate democratic values. Above all, there is a failure to insulate the electoral process from the influence of private wealth.

It is not a simple matter in a capitalist economy, particularly one with high levels of wealth and income inequality, to block the private use of wealth to influence politics in general and elections in particular. So long as capitalism remains dominant, it will generate levels of economic inequality that will spill into politics. But there are ways to dampen this effect. The key issue is to ensure the core funding for electoral politics is public rather than private. One way to accomplish this, proposed by Bruce Ackerman and Ian Ayers in their book *Voting with Dollars*, is to give every citizen a certain amount of money per year (perhaps in the form of a dedicated debit card)—say, $100—to spend on politics. Any person or political organization accepting funding through such direct citizen disbursements would be prevented from accepting any private money. This would provide an egalitarian distribution of democratic funding as a counterweight to the inequalities in private funding.

If it should come to pass that the democratic processes of the capitalist state were revitalized and deepened, then there would be a significant possibility of using the capitalist state to gradually erode the dominance of capitalism. Still, there is no guarantee whatsoever that such possibilities would be actually realized. Whether or not this happens depends on the capacity to struggle successfully for symbiotic reforms. This, in turn, raises the question: who is going to participate in such struggles? Where is the collective agent capable of sustaining struggles to erode capitalism? This is the subject of the next chapter.

6

Agents of Transformation

In some ways, the most vexing problem with the strategic vision of eroding capitalism is how to create collective actors with sufficient coherence and capacity for struggle to sustain the project of challenging capitalism. It is not enough to have a solid diagnosis and critique of the world as it is and a compelling account of the desirability and viability of alternatives that would make the world a better place. It is not even enough to map the strategies that would move us in the right direction. For those alternatives to actually be achievable, there must be political agents of transformation capable of bringing them about using those strategies. So, where are these collective actors?

I will begin by clarifying why collective actors are essential for any plausible strategy intended to erode capitalism. I will then discuss the notion of "agency" and three concepts that are central in the formation of collective actors: *identities*, *interests* and *values*. The rest of the chapter will explore the problem of how to navigate the complexities of creating effective collective actors for social transformation in the world today. I won't be able to provide a real answer to the question of where these collective actors are to be found, but I hope to clarify the task we confront in creating them.

Collective actors for eroding capitalism

To recall the central argument of Chapter 3, eroding capitalism combines four strategic logics: resisting capitalism, escaping capitalism, taming capitalism and dismantling capitalism. Different kinds of collective actors and coalitions of collective actors are involved in each of these.

Resisting capitalism is at the center of much of the labor movement and many social movements that confront the depredations of capitalism. Episodic mobilizations for protests and occupations designed to block austerity are contemporary examples. Escaping capitalism is a strategy for community activism anchored in the social and solidarity economy and in the cooperative market economy. Sometimes this can involve large federations of groups organized to foster noncapitalist forms of economic activities; sometimes the collective actors can be very small, taking advantage of local spaces that are available for creating noncapitalist economic relations.

Neither resisting nor escaping necessarily involves action primarily directed at gaining state power. In contrast, since both taming and dismantling capitalism seek to change the rules of the game, not simply move within existing rules, these strategies require political action to gain some measure of power within the state itself. Taming capitalism neutralizes harms of capitalism, especially through state-provided insurance of various sorts. Dismantling capitalism transfers certain aspects of property rights from private to public control, and removes the provision of certain kinds of goods and services from the market and the control of private investors. The pivotal logic of eroding capitalism, then, is that these changes in the rules of the game from above can expand the space for building alternatives to capitalist economic relations from below in ways that, over time, encroach on the dominance of capitalism.

One of the attractions of this strategic concoction is that it provides a legitimate place for very different kinds of activism that in different ways oppose the dominance of capitalism. Rather than seeing community activism around the social and solidarity economy and political activism over the state as antithetical, these can become complementary. In practical terms this is not always easy, of course, especially because the kinds of organizations needed for these different forms of anticapitalist strategy are so different. Nevertheless, they need not be viewed as intrinsically antagonistic.

The biggest puzzle in this argument on strategy for eroding capitalism concerns the creation of robust collective actors capable of acting politically to challenge and change capitalism's rules of the game in a progressive direction. Traditionally this has been the work of political parties. Other kinds of organizations and associations also play a role in politically directed action for progressive social change: lobbying organizations, interest organizations of all sorts, labor unions, community organizations, social movement organizations and many others. In some times and places, some of these organizations can have decisive effects on the prospects for progressive state action. But for these various kinds of civil society–based collective actors to have sustained efficacy in changing the rules enforced by the state, they need to somehow be connected to progressive political parties capable of acting directly within the state. Ultimately, then, the strategy of eroding capitalism depends on the existence of a web of collective actors anchored in civil society and political parties committed to such a political project.

The question, then, is how to think about the process of creating these kinds of interconnected collective actors capable of acting politically. To give more precision to this issue, we need to detour into a classic theme of social theory: the problem of collective agency.

The problem of collective agency

Social theory is filled with discussions of what is sometimes called the structure/agency problem. Much of this discussion is very abstract and often quite obscure. The issues are implicated in some of the big fault lines in social theory over things like methodological individualism versus systems theory, micro versus macro theory, contingency and determinacy, and the nature of explanation in social science. We won't explore these issues here. What we do need to do is clarify the idea of agency, especially "collective" agency, and then give some precision to the problem of creating effective collective actors for struggles against capitalism.

The concept of "agency"

As a general, abstract notion, the idea of "agency" refers to the fact that people, to use Göran Therborn's apt expression in his book *The Ideology of Power and the Power of Ideology* (Verso, 1980), are "conscious, reflecting initiators of acts in a structured, meaningful world." People are not simply programmed to follow scripts defined by roles; they instigate actions, often with considerable intelligence, creativity and improvisation. Of course, such agency occurs within all sorts of constraints, both those generated by the social structures within which people act and the internalized constraints embodied in beliefs and habits. Sometimes those constraints severely narrow the range of possible self-initiated actions; sometimes the constraints are looser. But human beings are never robots.

Social theorists and analysts vary in the extent to which human agency figures in their explanations of social phenomena. At one extreme are theorists, sometimes referred to as "structuralists," who come close to treating people as simply bearers of the social relations within which they live; for them, it is an illusion to think we are authors of our own acts. At the other extreme are theorists who come close to denying the explanatory relevance of social structures altogether. People are constituted by complex, intersecting subjectivities through which they form identities and act in the world.

In the present context, there is no need to sort out these very abstract issues. I will take it as given that people in fact are conscious initiators of actions, even if they are also creatures of unconscious habit and often act in highly scripted ways. This is critical, because unless people are agents in this sense, there really would be no point in writing books to clarify the harms generated by capitalism, the desirability of an alternative and the dilemmas of realizing those alternatives. The very possibility of strategy depends on people being conscious initiators of acts.

The idea of agency applies both to individuals and, in a more complex way, to collectivities. The shift from individuals to collective entities is another minefield in social theory, since collectivities don't "act" in exactly the same sense that individuals do. A statement like "the capitalist class opposed the New Deal" could mean "most capitalists opposed the New Deal" or "organizations and political parties representing the interests of the capitalist class opposed the New Deal," or "powerful members of the capitalist class, connected through social networks and private associations, opposed the New Deal and other capitalists generally went along with them"; but a "class" as such is not the sort of thing that is a conscious initiator of action. Collective actors have social bases, but the bases themselves are not "actors." When I refer to the agency of a collective actor, therefore, I will be referring to various kinds of organizations and associations through which people join together to cooperate in pursuit of their goals. Sometimes these can be tightly bounded organizations, like labor unions or political parties. Other times the idea of a collective actor applies to looser forms of goal-oriented cooperation, as in coalitions and alliances, or even broader concepts like "social movements." In all of these cases, the human persons who constitute the organizations, associations and coalitions are the real conscious initiators of action, but the fact that they have joined together to coordinate their actions through an organization means that their actions now have a collective, not simply individual, character.

Collective actors are critical for emancipatory social transformation. As noted in Chapter 3, much social change happens "behind the backs" of people as the unintended side effects of human action. But it is implausible that emancipatory social transformations that would better realize the values of equality/fairness, democracy/freedom and community/solidarity could simply be the cumulative unintended by-product of human action. Human emancipation, if it is to come about, requires strategy, and this implies agency. And since some of the targets of such strategy are powerful institutions, an effective strategy requires collective agency. So, again, where are the collective actors?

We need three more concepts to begin to explore this question: holding *identities, interests* and *values* as overlapping bases for the formation of collective actors. Identities are especially critical in forging solidarity within a collective actor; interests are central to shaping the objectives of collective action; values are important for connecting diverse identities and interests within common meanings.

Identities

The term *identity*, in its broadest sense, helps us understand how people classify themselves and others in terms of things that are salient in their lives. People have all sorts of identities, including those affiliated with their gender, race, class, sexual orientation, ethnicity, nationality, religion, language and physical disabilities, but also things like being a jazz lover, New Yorker, intellectual, long-distance runner, grandparent or having a specific political ideology. All of these (and many more) could appear in response to the question: what are the things that define who you are? The answer intrinsically has a dual character: any definition of who I am also defines which other people are like me. A person's identity, then, is a complex intersection of these kinds of categories.

Depending on the context, any one or a cluster of the elements in a particular person's identity profile could be subjectively the most salient to them. Consider a middle-class, Black, American, male jazz lover. There could be times and places in which being a jazz lover is what matters most in terms of this person's own sense of who they are and who they feel are kindred spirits, people like himself. Or consider a German secular intellectual of Jewish heritage. In 1925, being a German intellectual could have been their most salient identity. In 1935, being Jewish could have become the most salient.

This last example reveals something important about the idea of identity: Identities are not simply descriptive attributes of people that they find subjectively salient; they are closely linked to social relations and power. Here is a vignette that will clarify the issue.

In 2007, I spent a week in Sarajevo; I was invited by a group of undergraduates at the university who had organized a conference on the relevance of Marx and Hegel for contemporary issues. I stayed beyond the conference and gave a number of lectures and seminars on the themes of my work on *Real Utopias*. The students were eager and animated. They came from all three ethno-religious communities in Sarajevo—Bosnian Muslims, Croatian Catholics and Serbian Orthodox. They had all lived through the siege of Sarajevo as children and were fed up with ethno-nationalism. They desperately wanted to be cosmopolitan Europeans. By the end of the week, I felt very close to a number of them.

On the last evening we were in a pub together and I said, rather glibly, "You know, in terms of identity I feel much more like all of you than like American Christian Fundamentalists. They seem like they're from another planet. You are all kindred spirits, sharing my core values and sense of meaning."

A young woman in the group, in her early twenties, replied, "This is not what identity is all about. It is not an answer to the question 'Who am I?' It is the answer to the question, 'Who do other people say I am?' If we were to cross the bridge to the Serbian sector and there was a policeman who saw you get mugged, he would come to your rescue. If he saw me getting mugged, he would turn away."

Later she added, "It is a great privilege for people in rich countries with liberal democracies to be able to ask the question 'who am I?' rather than have their identities coercively imposed on them. The idea of young adults 'searching for their identity' just doesn't make as much sense here."

This story illustrates an important contrast among the many forms of identity that are subjectively salient to people: some of these mainly reflect differences among people, differences that matter to them and which to a greater or lesser extent they choose to cultivate, while others are imposed on them by the society in which they live. I had experienced the week in Sarajevo with these students as reflecting our common identity as progressive intellectuals, an identity that is chosen and cultivated over time. They experienced identity as something imposed on them by powerful forces over which they had little control. I had not recognized the inherently privileged position reflected in my view of identity as self-discovery.

Things are, of course, even more complicated than the simple contrast between imposed and cultivated identities. Many identities may be both imposed and cultivated. Ethnicity is a good example: the basic menu of ethnic identities may be given by the cultural practices of a society, and some of these may be imposed on people, but there can still be considerable variation in the extent to which the salience of a given ethnic identity is strengthened or weakened through individual and collective practices. At times, there are sharp struggles within an ethnic group over precisely this issue, especially when an ethnic identity is deeply connected to conflict with other ethnic groups. In the episodes of violent ethno-nationalist conflict in the aftermath of the disintegration of Yugoslavia in the 1990s, there were places in which there had been considerable intermarriage across ethnic lines and ethnic identities were quite subdued prior to the state's collapse. Political operatives engaged in acts of ethnic violence in order to create an atmosphere of fear across ethnic boundaries as a way of intensifying the salience of ethnic identities, which could then be used to form effective ethnically based collective actors. More generally, social movements grounded in imposed identities often spend considerable energy trying to strengthen and deepen the identities they are attempting to mobilize.

Identities play a critical role in the formation of collective actors because of the ways in which shared identity facilitates the solidarity needed for sustained collective action. Sustained collective action faces all sorts of obstacles. In particular, if people are motivated exclusively by narrow, personal self-interest, participation in collective action will often be experienced as costly in various ways. This can lead to what is called "free riding": sitting on the sidelines and letting other people do the work and bear the costs of participation in collective action. If, on the other hand, motivations are bound up with identities of fellow-feeling toward members of a group and a sense that "we're all in this together," then free riding may be a less pressing problem. Strong shared identities also can increase the sense of trust and predictability among potential participants in collective action and can therefore facilitate the formation of durable collective actors.

Identities that are rooted in various forms of socially imposed inequality and domination are especially salient for the formation of emancipatory collective actors. People live their lives within social structures not of their choosing; identities are, in significant ways, forged through their lived experiences within those structures. In particular, social structures are characterized by multiple forms of intersecting inequality, domination, exclusion and exploitation. These generate experiences of real harms in the lives of people—disrespect, deprivations, disempowerment, bodily insecurity and abuse. These experiences get transformed into shared identities through cultural interpretations, which, of course, are themselves objects of contestation. The aforementioned social bases of emancipatory social movements—class, race, gender, ethnicity, and so on—are deeply connected to these kinds of identities.

There is one additional feature of identity relevant to the forming of collective actors capable of contributing to emancipatory social transformation. Identities change over time, and one way that they change is through the effects of social struggles. The lived experience of participating in social movements and other forms of collective action can change a person's sense of who they are, what kind of person they are. Partially this is simply a spontaneous result of the shared experience of struggle, but of course it is also a result of the wide range of cultural and ideological practices that occur within social movements designed to cultivate changed identities. The result can be the formation of cultivated identities that are deeply connected to the collective actors in struggles—political parties, social movement organizations, labor unions—rather than simply to the categories that constitute the social base for those struggles.

Interests

Interests are connected to identities, but they are not the same thing. Identities are subjectively salient classifications of persons. Interests refer to things that would make a person's life go better along some dimension important to that person. Interests are anchored in the solutions to the problems people encounter in their lives; identities are anchored in the lived experiences generated in part by those problems. To say that a labor union is in the interests of workers is to assert that a union would make it easier to improve wages and working conditions for workers. To say that reduced government environmental regulation is in the interests of certain kinds of investors is to claim that the rate of return on their investments would be higher in the absence of regulation. A claim about interests, in a sense, is always a kind of prediction about the effects of alternative possibilities.

People can therefore be mistaken about their interests. Parents can believe, falsely, that vaccinations cause autism and are thus against the interests of their children. Lower-income people can believe that tax cuts for the rich will benefit the poor. This is the sense in which one can speak meaningfully about "false consciousness"—a false understanding of what in fact would make one's life better, about what specifically are the best means to realize some end. Claims about false consciousness are not in general claims about false *identity*. False consciousness describes incorrect beliefs about how the world actually works, which lead to incorrect views about the effects of different courses of action.

Some interests are closely tied to identities. A transgender person has specific interests about the ways culturally recognized gender classifications affect access to various kinds of amenities and resources. A linguistic minority in a country has specific interests about the official standing of different languages, as well as policies around language use and education. A person with a strong Catholic identity may have specific interests about policies that would prevent abortions. Other interests are not so closely grounded in specific identities. The interests people have in policies that would reduce carbon emissions and mitigate climate change are not simply the interests of people with identities as environmentalists. And the interests that broad masses of people have in economic democracy are not closely linked to their specific identities within capitalist class relations.

Because of the complexity of lives and identities, people have many different interests, which are often in tension, even incompatible. People have interests linked to their class location, gender, health status, religion, ethnicity, nationality, language, sexuality. They also have short-run interests and long-term interests, which may also be in tension. As a result, when people think about what is in their interests, they inevitably have to foreground some interests and bracket others. A central issue in political struggles is precisely over which interests should be given the greatest attention.

Values

When we say that people are "conscious, reflecting initiators of acts in a structured, meaningful world" we are not merely saying that they consciously initiate acts, but that they do so in a "meaningful world." A key part of an action's meaning involves values—the beliefs people hold about what is good, both in terms of how people should behave in the world and how our social institutions should function.

Values have a fraught relationship to interests. When political conservatives defend tax cuts for the rich by saying that, through increasing investment and thus economic growth, this is the best way to help the poor, they are invoking a general social value: poverty is a bad thing and a good society is one in which the lives of the least advantaged improve over time. Most people would agree with this affirmation of values. *If* it were true that cutting taxes for the rich was the best way to help the poor, this would be a powerful reason to support such policies. Of course, this view of tax cuts is a rationalization for the interests of the rich. It is often relatively easy to invoke broadly shared values as a cover for self-interest. This happens on the left as well—for example, when authoritarian states used the banner of communism to claim to be democratic and ruled by the people. It is only because values are important to people that this ideological strategy of mystification works.

Values have always played a crucial role in emancipatory struggles. White students who went to the southern United States to help register African Americans to vote during Freedom Summer in 1964 did so not because this was in their interests, but because of commitment to values of equality, democracy and solidarity. The movement in the United States and Europe during the anti-apartheid struggle to boycott participation in events in South Africa and to divest universities and other institutions of investments in South Africa was not because of the interests of participants, but because of their values. Of course, people also join social struggles because the goals are in their interests, but moral commitments and values help to reinforce their participation and widen the appeal of the cause.

Values can thus be powerful sources of motivation. Crucially, they can themselves become a robust source of identity. When those values are integrated into more or less systematic bodies of thought, they can be thought of as a dimension of ideologies. Emancipatory ideologies combine explanations for how the world works, account for what alternatives are possible, and affirm values. Such ideologies can be highly elaborate or loosely constructed; often, they are filled with internal inconsistencies. But even with inconsistencies, ideologies can become important dimensions of people's identities.

From identities, interests and values to collective actors

Identities, interests and values do not spontaneously precipitate the formation of collective actors, let alone politically organized collective actors capable of contributing to emancipatory social transformation. While it is always the case that people have identities, interests and values that they hold in common with others, these need not be translated into coherent forms of collective organization. What is more, which aspects—if any—of a person's identity are translated into solidarity and which interests and values garner their attention depends heavily on the presence of preexisting collective actors attempting to mobilize identities in pursuit of interests and values. This is a kind of chicken-and-egg problem: identities are critical for the formation of collective actors, but collective actors play an active role in strengthening the salience of particular identities. Social struggles are often precisely over competing bases trying to mobilize the same people: class or nationality or religion, for example. And of course, most people live their private lives disengaged from any significant involvement in organized collective action, whether political or civic.

This is the terrain on which any political project for eroding capitalism must operate. This terrain poses three main challenges to the task of constructing collective actors capable of sustained political action: 1. overcoming privatized lives; 2. building class solidarity within complex, fragmented class structures; 3. forging anticapitalist politics in the presence of diverse, competing non–class-based forms of identity.

Overcoming privatized lives

Most people usually live their lives in networks of family, work and community, dealing with the practical matters of everyday life without being mobilized into the base of support for any politically oriented collective actor. The tasks of daily life, especially once one has a family and children, take enormous amounts of time, energy and attention. It is not surprising that it is young people, often less encumbered by such responsibilities, who fuel protest movements and political mobilizations.

The gulf between private lives and public involvement is always a problem. It is made more difficult in a consumerist society, where people are led to believe that personal happiness and well-being depend largely on one's level of personal consumption, especially when this is combined with highly competitive labor markets, in which the acquisition of the means of private consumption depends on one's ability to compete with others.

Taken together, the universal issue of time and energy constraints for individuals living their lives and the more specific issues of consumerism and competitive individualism create a difficult environment for mobilizing coherent political collective actors in contemporary capitalist countries. These difficulties historically have been somewhat mitigated by various kinds of civic associations, which integrate with people's daily lives. In many places, two such associations have played especially salient roles: labor unions and churches. Unions, where they are strong, form a robust bridge between politics and workers' daily lives. It is no coincidence that progressive political parties critical of capitalism typically have strong ties to labor movements. Churches, in different times and places, have also played this sort of role, although more often for conservative than for progressive politics. People gather in church as part of their ordinary lives. They talk to each other at church functions. They share a salient identity anchored in religion. And sometimes churches become directly involved in political organizing, helping overcome the purely private concerns of their members by linking religious identities to political interests. Black southern churches in the United States played this role for progressive politics during the civil rights era. Today, white evangelical churches play this role in overcoming the apolitical, privatized lives of their members by linking religious identities to right-wing politics.

Fragmented class structures

Class is at the very heart of the strategic configuration of eroding capitalism. Eroding capitalism means undermining the dominance of capitalism over time within the overall economic ecosystem, and this means undermining the power of capitalists. The most natural social base for such struggles are those people within class relations who are directly subjected to capitalist domination and exploitation, the working class. The lived experience of domination and exploitation of workers within capitalist relations could provide a congenial context for forging strong working-class identities. The identity-interests of workers would then form the core of progressive politics that embraced the more universal interests linked to values of equality, democracy and solidarity.

As noted, in the middle of the nineteenth century, Marx believed that the underlying dynamics of capitalism would push people in capitalist societies in this direction. In particular, he believed that over time the class structure of capitalism would become increasingly simplified, with the vast majority of people sharing relatively homogeneous conditions of existence, making the task of class identity formation easier. Ideological struggles would still be needed to get workers to understand the causes of their common lived experience of suffering under capitalism, but changes in the underlying class structure would make this task easier. The working class would become over time the coherent social base for a powerful political collective actor organized against capitalism. The aspiration of this prediction is captured in the famous last sentences of the *Communist Manifesto*, "The proletarians have nothing to lose but their chains. They have a world to win. Working Men of All Countries, Unite!"

This is not how the class structure of capitalism has developed over the last 150 years. Instead of increasing homogenization of the working class, the class structure has become more complex in ways that undercut the shared sense of fate and life conditions. While it may be true that income distributions in many advanced capitalist countries have become considerably more polarized in recent decades, which fueled the slogan "we are the 99%," it is not the case the 99 percent share a common lived experience. Even if we take the subset of that 99 percent consisting of wage earners selling their labor power in the labor market—the broadly defined working class—there is a pervasive fragmentation of lived experience that makes a common class identity difficult to forge. To list only a few of these complexities, the lived experiences of workers vary enormously in terms of level and security of earnings; precariousness of employment; autonomy within work; skill levels and education required within work; opportunities for creativity; and so on.

To use the game metaphor framework from Chapter 3, the working class may share common interests at the level of "the game"—economic democracy as an emancipatory alternative to capitalism would make life better for all workers—but at the level of the rules and, even more so, moves in the game, the working class is fragmented with divergent interests. Economic struggles within capitalism are waged largely over game moves and rules, and thus such struggles often intensify rather than mute these divisions. Many people still experience class as a salient identity, but it does not provide the universalizing basis for solidarity for which progressives once hoped.

Competing sources of identity

The third major challenge to forging politically robust anticapitalist collective actors concerns the heterogeneity of salient sources of identity in people's lives. Here is the problem: anticapitalism is, at its heart, a class project, but class identities must compete in various ways with all sorts of other identities as the basis for emancipatory collective action.

As a first approximation, we can distinguish two situations: Some non-class identities themselves constitute distinct bases for emancipatory struggle and have the potential to be constituent elements of progressive politics; other non-class identities generate interests hostile to emancipatory alternatives to existing social structures and institutions, and thus constitute obstacles.

One of the hallmarks of progressive politics in recent decades has been the importance of identities rooted in the lived experience of domination, inequality and exclusion other than class. The familiar contemporary examples include race, ethnicity, gender and sexuality. Social movements and other forms of collective actors anchored in these identities have often been more prominent politically than explicitly class-based anticapitalist collective actors.

The interests directly linked to these non-class identities are not the same as class interests, but the *values* connected to those interests overlap with the values of emancipatory anticapitalism. Consider identities rooted in racial oppression. Oppressed racial minorities have identity-interests in ending racial discrimination and domination. These are not the same as working-class interests. Sometimes, indeed, there are tensions between the identity-interests of racial minorities and the identity-interests of workers, as when struggles against racial discrimination affect the immediate conditions of labor market competition for white workers. Yet both sets of interests share the egalitarian value of equal access to the material and social means necessary to live a flourishing life. Similarly, for the harms linked to oppressions tied to gender and sexuality: these harms generate distinct identity-interests, but they share the same fundamental egalitarian value as emancipatory anticapitalism. Values, then, constitute a potential basis for constructing political unity across these diverse identities.

Any effort at constructing a robust anticapitalist collective actor has to navigate the complexity of these multiple, intersecting identities that share common underlying emancipatory values but nevertheless have distinct identity-interests. A potentially much more difficult problem concerns non-class identities whose identity-interests are deeply hostile to the values associated with anticapitalism. In the first decades of the twenty-first century, of particular salience throughout the developed capitalist world are identities rooted in racial dominance and exclusionary nationalism. What has come to be known as "right-wing populism" mobilizes people on the basis of interests tied to such exclusionary identities. The attraction of significant segments of the working class to this kind of political formation is a direct challenge to the prospects of any form of emancipatory anticapitalism.

It is easy—but, I think, a mistake—to see this upsurge of right-wing populism as tapping into widespread, virulent racist and exclusionary nationalist identities. To be sure, there are undoubtedly people drawn to these political movements whose core identities are deeply hostile to racial minorities, immigrants and others. But for many, perhaps most, people who end up supporting right-wing populist politics, these aspects of identity become foregrounded as a result of the political context and lack of available alternatives. Beginning in the 1990s, the political parties traditionally linked to the working class generally embraced, to varying degrees, the core idea of neoliberalism: wherever possible, markets and private initiatives should replace direct state programs as ways of fostering economic dynamism and solving social problems. The disillusionment with the capacity of those parties to improve the lives of most working-class people creates a political vacuum that allows right-wing populism to gain traction. So, while exclusionary nationalism and racism are part of the cultural landscape of identities in most places, the extent to which they are foregrounded or subdued depends on politics.

Real politics

The formation of effective politically organized collective actors is essential for eroding capitalism. And everywhere, political activists attempting to build collective actors opposed to capitalism face the obstacles of privatized lives, fragmented class structures and competing identities. These are universal issues. The practical challenges of how best to overcome these obstacles, however, are highly context-dependent, varying enormously over time and place.

Competitive individualism as a feature of broadly shared culture is more salient in the United States than in many other countries, and it intensifies the challenges created by privatized lives. Even within developed capitalist countries, there is significant variation in the intensity and forms of class structure fragmentation, the extent and distribution of precariousness, and the degree of inequality within the working class. The importance of racism as a salient obstacle to forming robust progressive political collective actors clearly varies across countries. It has been historically noteworthy in the United States, although in recent decades, with the rapid increase in immigration from Africa and the Middle East to Europe, racism has become increasingly salient there as well, especially in the face of the refugee crisis created by Middle East wars. In mid-twentieth-century Europe, fighting racism was not a central problem faced by anticapitalist actors in most places; today it is. In these and other ways, then, the challenges posed by privatized lives, fragmented class structures and competing identities vary.

Furthermore, in addition to these variations in social context for the formation of collective actors, there is enormous variation across countries' political institutions, within which progressive political activists operate. These deeply shape the practical problems activists face in forming collective political actors. This is especially critical for building the long-term political capacity to effectively compete for state power within electoral politics, as eroding capitalism requires being able to use the state to tame capitalism and, in incremental ways, dismantle key aspects of capitalist economic relations. Protests and mobilizations outside of the state may be effective in blocking certain state policies; they are not by themselves effective in robustly changing the rules of the game in progressive ways. For this to happen, external protests must be linked to political parties able to pass needed legislation and implement new game rules. And this requires political parties capable of competing effectively in electoral politics.

The process of creating this political capacity is deeply affected by political rules of the game, including:

- *Rules governing political representation*: winner-take-all, single-member districts; single-member districts with runoff elections, including instant runoffs; various forms of proportional representation; nonpartisan elections (especially at the local level); and so on.
- *Rules governing the drawing of boundaries of electoral districts*: party-controlled gerrymandering; independent commissions.
- *Rules governing the selection of candidates*: systems in which political parties control the selection of candidates; primary election systems in which voters select candidates; nonpartisan elections in which candidates get on the ballot through petition signatures.
- *Rules governing campaign finance*: the degree of restriction on private financing of elections, including prohibitions on contributions by corporations; various forms of public finance.
- *Rules governing eligibility to vote*: automatic registration of all adult citizens; various rules that restrict or suppress voter registration (felon disenfranchisement; voter ID laws; voter list purges; and so on).

These rules (and others) significantly affect the tasks and dilemmas faced by progressive activists in trying to expand the capacity for effective political collective action. Should anticapitalist, progressive activists work within established left and center-left parties, or form new parties? Should their efforts be concentrated at local, regional or national levels of political contestation? What sorts of ties should there be between progressive social movements and political parties? Because of the complexity and variability both in social context and political institutions, there can be no general formula to answer these questions.

While there is no general formula, there are nonetheless some guidelines we can formulate from our analysis for forming collective actors to effectively erode capitalism.

First, the discussion of values should be at the very center of progressive politics. The three clusters of values discussed in Chapter 1—equality/fairness, democracy/ freedom and community/solidarity—should be made explicit and explained. Discussions of values, of course, can become high-sounding but empty window dressing. It is important to emphasize how these values relate to the concrete policies that advance radical economic democracy.

Second, these values can provide a vital connection between the class interests at the heart of eroding capitalism and other identity-interests with emancipatory aspirations. What has been termed the "identity politics" of oppressed social categories should be treated as an integral element within a broad emancipatory politics rather than a matter of secondary concern. The task for progressive anticapitalists attempting to build a politics intended to erode the dominance of capitalism is to include explicit reform programs that recognize these identity-interests and connect them to the agenda of eroding capitalism, especially through actively valuing equal access to the social and material conditions necessary to live a flourishing life.

Third, the value of democracy, at least at this time, should be given particular emphasis in articulating the concrete program of progressive politics. A deeper democracy, real democracy, is in the interests of a very broad part of the population beyond the working class. The thinness of democracy within capitalist states constitutes one of the principal obstacles to advancing policies that reduce capitalism's dominance, but efforts to restore and deepen democracy also constitute a unifying objective for people who may be less sympathetic to the overall anticapitalist agenda.

Fourth, it is important to remember that the overall plan of eroding capitalism is not exclusively state-centered, and political parties are not the only collective actors needed for this strategy to be carried out. Eroding capitalism depends as much on resisting and escaping capitalism as on the concentrated politics of taming and dismantling it. In particular, the efforts at building and expanding the social and solidarity economy, the cooperative market economy and the array of new economic practices opened up by IT-enabled relations, such as peer-to-peer collaborative production, are essential for this long-term erosion. Recall that eroding capitalism means both encroaching on it by reversing the privatization of the provision of public goods and services by the state and expanding the diverse forms of noncapitalist economic activity outside the state. New technological developments, which reduce economies of scale and facilitate cooperation, will likely increase the growth of these noncapitalist ways of organizing economic life. Recognizing the importance of these initiatives from below, and formulating reform policies that would expand the economic space for their growth, would also deepen the social base for the broader agenda of eroding capitalism.

In developed capitalist democracies today, there is a widespread sense that the political-economic system is not working well, perhaps even unraveling. Both the state and economy seem incapable of responding coherently and creatively to the challenges we face, whether it involves adapting to the ramifications of climate change, let alone mitigating its underlying causes; the global refugee crisis, which is likely to intensify in the coming decades as climate refugees are added to war refugees and economic migrants; increasing economic polarization within wealthy countries; the prospect of either a "jobless" future caused by automation and artificial intelligence, or at best a future in which market-generated jobs are either well paid and demanding very high levels of education and knowledge, or are badly paid, precarious positions. Capitalism as it exists today is a major obstacle to effectively dealing with all of these issues.

One reaction to these trends is gloom and doom. Capitalism seems unassailable. The disarray, and in some places the disintegration, of traditional political parties, has generated a sense of political incompetence and paralysis. This has created the opening for right-wing, nativist populism. One can easily imagine a future in which the erosion of liberal democracy accelerates and slides into much more authoritarian, if still nominally democratic, forms of government. Such developments are already apparent in some capitalist democracies on the periphery of western Europe. This could certainly happen as well in what had been thought to be the most stable liberal democracies.

But this is not the only possibility. Capitalism as it currently exists need not be our future. Popular disaffection with capitalism is widespread even in the absence of confidence in the viability of an alternative system. Resilient efforts at escaping the depredations of corporate capitalism by building new ways of organizing our economic life can be found everywhere. And there are serious efforts at creating new political formations, sometimes within traditional parties on the left, sometimes in the form of new parties. The potential for constructing a broad social base for a new era of progressive politics exists. The contingencies of historical events and the creative agency of activists and collective actors will determine whether this potential is realized.

Erik Olin Wright (1947–2019)

Afterword

by Michael Burawoy

In the early hours of January 23, 2019, one of the great social scientists of our era stopped breathing. At seventy-one, he died at the height of his influence. Tributes poured in from all over the world: from politicians and activists; from collaborators and colleagues; from students, past and present; from people who knew him and those who didn't. Tributes to his humanity as well as his intellectual brilliance.

Erik Olin Wright had been battling acute myeloid leukemia for ten months, balancing his characteristic optimism with a fearless realism. Even as his life was ebbing away, he didn't stop fighting for a better future. He set about writing a long letter to his grandchildren; he was concerned that his students be well cared for, intellectually and materially; he worried about the future of his department at the University of Wisconsin, which had been his academic home for forty-two years. He wanted the Havens Center, now the Havens Wright Center, to outlive him—the center he had founded and directed for thirty-five years, hosting progressive thinkers from all over the world. And, of course, he never lost interest in exploring capitalism's possible futures. He held out hope for a new generation of socialists, encouraged by the youthful magazine *Jacobin* that had enthusiastically published his paper on anticapitalism. As he was dying, he watched with hope the ascendancy of Alexandria Ocasio-Cortez and the Democratic Socialists of America. To that last breath, he remained an optimist and a real utopian. It's all captured in his soulful blog read by hundreds, following the ups and downs of his last ten months.

Before he became a radical Marxist, Erik had been influenced at Harvard by the structural functionalism of Talcott Parsons and at Oxford by the political sociology of Steven Lukes and the social history of Christopher Hill, receiving a bachelor's degree from each institution. To avoid the Vietnam War draft, he enrolled as a student at the Unitarian Theological Seminary in Berkeley. There he ran his own seminar on utopia and revolution—a theme to which he would return twenty years later. In 1971, staying in Berkeley, he entered the PhD program in the sociology department at the University of California. For his generation of Berkeley graduate students, Marxism and sociology formed a prickly marriage, at once partners and antagonists. Erik and his fellow graduate students started their own parallel curriculum devoted to Marxist social science, connected to such local journals as *Kapitalistate* and *Socialist Revolution*.

Marxism turned sociology upside down. The study of stratification and status became the study of class relations. Political sociology turned from a fixation on liberal democracy to theories of the capitalist state, and from totalitarian theory to the class character of state socialism; economic sociology turned from the verities of industrialism to the dynamics of capitalism; organization theory turned from hollow generalities to the study of the capitalist labor process; the sociology of education turned from research into learning to the reproduction of class; the irrationality of collective behavior was replaced by the rationality of social movements; studies of race prejudice and race cycle theories were displaced by studies of racial oppression and internal colonialism; modernization theory gave way to world systems analysis and critiques of imperialism; under the sway of socialist feminism the sociology of the family moved its focus from socialization to reproductive labor, from gender roles to a ubiquitous patriarchy. In short, Marxist theory replaced abstruse structural functionalism; the critique of US society replaced sociology's self-satisfied celebration of American society. In 1970, Alvin Gouldner had correctly anticipated "the coming crisis of western sociology" but what he didn't anticipate was the Marxist renaissance of sociology.

Erik would play a major part in bringing excitement back to sociology. Together with his close Italian friend Luca Perrone, whom he would lose in a tragic diving accident, Erik developed his famous scheme of contradictory class locations that enabled Marxists to go beyond the fundamental capital-labor binary to include petty bourgeoisie, small employers, managers and supervisors, and professionals. He debuted this nuanced breakdown of class structure simultaneously in the leading English-language Marxist journal, *New Left Review*, and the dominant professional sociology journal, the *American Sociological Review*. He then elaborated a fully fledged Marxist rewriting of sociology in *Class, Crisis and the State* (New Left Books, 1978). It was a book that took the disobedient generation by storm—a unique joining of innovative theory, tough empiricism, and logical argumentation. It was a Marxist genre that had not been seen before.

Sociology and Marxism were not only antagonists; they were also competitors. Erik set out to demonstrate that his class schema better explained inequality, in particular income inequality, than the stratification models of sociologists, the human capital models of economists, and even the Marxist schemas of Nicos Poulantzas, which were much in vogue at the time. Erik's success took on a momentum of its own. Soon he obtained funds to field national surveys and thereby created maps of class structure and measures of class consciousness, inspiring parallel projects in over fifteen countries across the globe. He had used the tools of social science to replace conventional paradigms with novel ways to think about capitalism.

At the same time as he began measuring class and its effects, he joined a group of distinguished philosophers and social scientists who called themselves Analytical Marxists. Their purpose was to rid Marxism of so-called bullshit—what they considered to be philosophical mumbo jumbo, leaps of logic, or wishful thinking—to produce a rigorous science, often based on methodological individualism or rational choice theory. Even when most of the members had turned away from Marxism, the modus operandi of this group remained, until the end of his life, indelibly engraved in all that Erik wrote. Early on in the 1980s Erik was greatly influenced by John Roemer, a leading contributor to no-bullshit Marxism, and his innovative theory of exploitation. This led Erik to turn his theory of contradictory class locations into a conceptualization of class around the distribution of different assets: labor power, means of production, organizational assets, and skill assets. If feudalism was based on the unequal distribution of labor power, capitalism was based on the unequal distribution of the means of production; statism on the unequal distribution of organizational assets; and communism on the unequal distribution of skills. This became the basis of his important book *Classes* (Verso, 1985).

At the same time, he agreed to work with sociologists in the Soviet Union, who didn't want to be left out of the burgeoning international comparisons of class structure. So, in 1986 I went with Erik to Moscow and was able to witness the Soviet academics' reaction to what must have appeared to them a very puzzling creature—a Western Marxist with an indefatigable commitment to science. We sat down with the Soviet team to develop a parallel survey instrument that could be fielded in both countries. What strange and frustrating meetings they were, as we stumbled on elementary methodological disputes and struggled to develop questions that would mean the same in both the United States and the USSR. At the end of the visit Erik was invited to address social scientists at the Academy of Sciences. I remember the waves of suppressed panic and elation—these were after all the years of Perestroika and Glasnost—that swept through the packed audience as Erik unfurled his new theory of class. They could see only too clearly that, with his calm and unassuming delivery and the piercing clarity of his language, Erik was unmistakably arguing that organizational exploitation was at the heart of the Soviet order. The talk was abruptly shut down.

As the 1980s wore on, Erik became increasingly aware of being trapped by his very success and by the methods he employed. He had developed what his students called, somewhat ironically, multiple-regression Marxism, using the latest statistical techniques to calculate the influence of objective class position on various subjective orientations—all derived from survey research. The culminating volume in this research program was *Class Counts: Comparative Studies in Class Analysis* (Cambridge University Press, 1997). He inscribed the copy he gave me: "Alas, see what has become of revolutionary dialectics."

Erik would never be totally liberated from the research program on class analysis he had initiated, but in 1991 he began his new journey into real utopias. This, too, was decisively shaped by the critical and foundational thought of Analytical Marxism. The Marxist bubble had already burst, the collapse of the Soviet Union supposedly spelled the end of Marxism—though Erik saw it as the liberation of Marxism from the stranglehold of a degenerate Soviet ideology. Capitalism was riding high in the Western world, and Margaret Thatcher was convincing many that there was no alternative. Erik took this as a challenge to forge a new Marxism—one that defied its historic hostility to utopian thinking.

The idea was to seek out institutional forms based in reality, lodged within the interstices of capitalism, whose organizational principles were at odds with capitalism. In collaboration with the journal *Politics and Society*, with which he had been associated since 1979, Erik sought out authors who possessed an imaginative design for an alternative world. He worked with them to design their own particular real utopia and then organized a conference around the vision. Verso published each conference as a collection Erik edited. So far six volumes have appeared, covering collectively the following topics: associational democracy, market socialism, recasting egalitarianism, deepening democracy, basic income grants, and gender equality. When he died he had been hard at work developing a volume on the cooperative economy, after holding conferences in Argentina, South Africa, Spain, and Italy. Real utopias had become a global project.

In 2010 Verso published Erik's magnum opus, *Envisioning Real Utopias*. It had been twenty years in the making. He called it a research program in emancipatory social science. It sets out from a diagnosis of the ills of capitalism to call for a better world, a socialism that is both viable and feasible. No longer based on an illusory breakdown of capitalism nor a tyrannical form of state planning, the goal was to restore the "social in socialism" —the empowerment of civil society, first against the state through such institutional designs as participatory budgeting or citizen assemblies, and second against the economy through such programs as universal basic income or cooperatives. Each real utopia is examined for its conditions of existence, possibilities of dissemination, and its internal contradictions.

When it came to the realization of real utopias, he considered three ways forward. First, there was ruptural transformation, which he demoted in favor of symbiotic and interstitial transformations.

Symbiotic transformation refers to the reformist road in which short-term concessions to solve capitalist crises sow the seeds of socialism. An example would be class compromise, which incorporates the working class but plants the idea of collective appropriation of capital, such as the Swedish Meidner-Hedborg Plan. Welfare for all raises the possibility of universal basic income that would create spaces for alternative forms of production as well as challenging capitalist power in the workplace.

Interstitial transformation, on the other hand, refers to the development of alternative institutions within the framework of capitalist society, such as cooperatives or peer-to-peer collaboration in the digital world. Libraries and Wikipedia were among Erik's favorite real utopias.

Erik had originally intended *Envisioning Real Utopias* for a broad audience, but as he wrestled with his critics, it became both more voluminous and more complex, addressing a more specialized audience. As he toured the world, however, speaking about his book he increasingly commanded the interest of political activists. This was something new and exciting. So, he set about writing a new version, which would appear in two volumes: one a popular manual; the other a more academic debate. He began the first volume in 2016 and by the time he was diagnosed with leukemia had completed all but the last chapter.

How to Be an Anticapitalist in the Twenty-First Century recaps, in succinct and incisive language, many of the arguments of *Envisioning Real Utopias*, but it also represents a shift in his thinking. Erik begins forthrightly with four theses: first, another world is possible; second, it could improve conditions of human flourishing for most people; third, elements of this world are already being created; and, finally, there are ways to move from here to there. As in *Envisioning Real Utopias* he advances a diagnosis of capitalism's ills, only instead of an arbitrary list of defects, he organizes the critique of capitalism around the violation of three pairs of values: equality/fairness, democracy/ freedom, and community/solidarity. Together, these values form the normative foundations of democratic socialism.

From here he turns to the strategic logics of anticapitalism. Again, he frames this differently than in the previous book. He dismisses "smashing the state"—you can never build the new out of the ashes of the old—but he does embrace "dismantling" capitalism (installing elements of socialism from above) and "taming" capitalism (neutralizing its harms). These strategies from above are complemented by strategies from below: "resisting" capitalism and "escaping" capitalism. It is the articulation of these four strategies that brings about the "eroding" of capitalism—his reformulation of the transition to democratic socialism.

We live in a capitalist ecosystem composed of a variety of capitalist and noncapitalist organizations and institutions.

Capitalist relations dominate, but don't monopolize the ecosystem. The transition to a democratic socialism involves deepening the noncapitalist elements and turning them into anticapitalist elements that include the familiar list: unconditional basic income that creates space for other forms of production—the solidarity economy and the cooperative economy; disempowering capital through the democratization of the firm and the creation of public banks; nonmarket economic organizations such as the state provision of goods and services and peer-to-peer collaborative production.

This strategy of erosion, this rearticulation of the different constituents of the capitalist ecosystem, necessarily involves the state, being as it is the cement of the whole social formation. Here, too, Erik departs from the Marxist orthodoxy that treats the state as a coherent object wielded by the capitalist class or a coherent subject that somehow always acts in the interests of capitalism. Instead, he presents the capitalist state as a heterogeneous, internally contradictory entity, one that reflects the diversity of the capitalist ecosystem. There are fissures and tensions within and among the agencies that can act as a lever for deepening democracy.

After being diagnosed with cancer, Erik had still to complete the last chapter of this book, the most difficult chapter, tackling the question everyone had been asking him. Who is going to forge the path to democratic socialism? Just like Marx, who died still stuck on the question of class, so, in his last months, Erik would wrestle once again with the question of human agency. While he is very clear that democratic socialism will not arise without collective struggle, he doesn't come down on a particular agent or combination of agents. Instead, he analyzes the conditions for such a struggle—the importance of *identities* that can forge solidarities, *interests* that lead to realistic objectives, and *values* that can create political unity across diverse identities and interests. He cannot identify any one particular agent of transformation.

Here lies the answer to the conundrum of Erik Wright's oeuvre: namely his move from class analysis without utopias to utopias without class analysis. *How to Be an Anticapitalist in the Twenty-First Century* offers an answer to this puzzle. It is one thing to be anticapitalist, he argues, but it is another thing to be a democratic socialist. Class struggle can contribute to the former but is inadequate for the latter. Where Marx considered an inevitable class polarization would lead to the magical coincidence of the demise of capitalism and the building of socialism, Erik draws the conclusion from his own class analysis that by itself class is too fragmented and limited a social force to build something new. If "eroding capitalism" is not to lead to barbarism but to democratic socialism, the transformation will require moral vision to propel struggles for a better world. He backs the troika: equality, democracy, and solidarity.

But who will be gripped by such values? One of Erik's most remarkable traits was the capacity to persuade through logical argument. Famous for the speed and clarity of his mind, Erik achieved a rare following—for an academic—among activists, who saw in his real utopias affirmation for their arduous projects. Possessed of an unlimited capacity to render his ideas precise and simple, without diluting them, Erik gave activists a vision of a collective project to which each could contribute. Given the resurgent interest in "socialism" among a new generation of critical thinkers and activists, Erik had an ever-increasing following. Although he's no longer around to make the argument for socialism in person, there are still many of his videos on YouTube, and now there's a powerful manifesto in *How to Be an Anticapitalist in the Twenty-First Century*. Unlike *The Communist Manifesto*, it does not prophesy or prefigure who will make a better— more equal, more democratic, more solidary—world but rather itself will shape and inspire activists to forge such a new socialism. The concrete phantasies he points to will create their own agents of realization.

Erik's last book reminds me of classical sociology. Emile Durkheim ended his sociology-defining text *The Division of Labor in Society* (1893) with the following words:

> In short, our first duty at the present time is to fashion a morality for ourselves. Such a task cannot be improvised in the silence of the study. It can arise only of its own volition, gradually, and under pressure of internal causes that render it necessary. What reflection can and must do is to prescribe the goal that must be attained. That is what we have striven to accomplish.

Durkheim embraced variants of the same values as Wright —freedom, justice, and solidarity—goals to be achieved through a form of guild socialism. But Durkheim offers no understanding as to how his socialism would be realized because he never conceived, let alone studied, the obstacle that is capitalism. By thematizing capitalism and the strategies for its transformation, by delineating concrete institutions that could carry us forward, Erik Wright gave us a Marxism that was sociology's final conclusion and ultimate critique, a practical and theoretical project that would invite everyone to forge a better world.

May 2019